When You Can
You Will

When You Can You Will

WHY YOU CAN'T ALWAYS DO WHAT YOU WANT TO DO . . . AND WHAT TO DO ABOUT IT

Lynne Bernfield, M.A., M.F.C.T.

LOWELL HOUSE
Los Angeles
CONTEMPORARY BOOKS
Chicago

Library of Congress Cataloging-in-Publication Data

Bernfield, Lynne.
    When you can you will : why you can't always do what you
want to do . . . and what to do about it / Lynne Bernfield.
        p.   cm.
    Includes bibliographical references and index.
    ISBN 1-56565-008-5
    1. Change (Psychology)   I. Title.
BF637.C4B46   1992
158'.1—dc20   92-20027
                                                          CIP

Requests for such permissions should be addressed to:

Lowell House
2029 Century Park East, Suite 3290
Los Angeles, CA 90067
Publisher: Jack Artenstein
Executive Vice-President: Nick Clemente
Vice-President/Editor-in-Chief: Janice Gallagher
Director of Publishing Services: Mary D. Aarons
Design: Tanya Maiboroda

Manufactured in the United States of America
10 9 8 7 6 5 4 3 2 1

Contents

This book is dedicated
to possibilities;
to the corner around which,
no matter how hard we try, we cannot see;
to life.

Acknowledgments

First and foremost I'd like to thank my clients, those remarkable people who shared with me their deepest secrets, their pain and suffering as well as their strength and courage. It is from them that I learned over and over again to trust the wisdom of the unconscious, to wait for the magic of readiness, and to honor and respect the self-protective impulse not to change.

Writing this book has been a wonderful experience. From the beginning I received encouragement, support, help, guidance, and the generous sharing of expertise, information, and resources. There was always an ear, an eye, or a shoulder when I needed it. All the people I mention here were important to me and without some this book could quite literally never have been.

My family: my parents, who have always loved, encouraged, and believed in me; my sister and brother, who are my best friends and my closest allies in my quest to be whole; my multitalented husband, who thinks I can do anything; my stepdaughter, who massaged my computer-weary muscles.

My friends and colleagues: Bob Arnold, Laura Golden-Bellotti, Anne Bowen, Don Buday, Victor Byrd, Carol Cellucci, Bob Chambers, Pamela Grant, Joyce Sunilla-Holt, Halina Irving, Carole Schweid, Sydnee Balaber-Smith, Merry Sanders, Diana Walker, and Kathy Wexler, some of whom read, read, and reread, some of whom offered the kindness and sympathy which sustained me, and who between them have, know, or know how to get everything.

The crew at Lowell House: Mary Aarons, Nick Clemente, Fred Goss, Peter Hoffman, Lisa Lenthall, and Bud Sperry, who, on my behalf, did more than their jobs and made me feel like a part of the team instead of a pain in the neck.

And most especially, Susan Schulman, not only an agent but an advocate; Janice Gallagher, not only a publisher but a champion; and Molly Maguire-Silverman, not only an editor but a mind reader.

Thank You.

You Can't
Hurry Change

———

This is a book about change, but what I say here may surprise you; it may be the very opposite of what you believe about what fosters and what deters change. You may think that wanting and trying should be enough to make change happen. You may think that you should be able to bring about any change at any time, or that inability to change is a weakness, a fault, a failure, "copping out," or proof that you're bad. When you can't effect a desired change, you may accuse yourself of being self-destructive.

I don't believe that human beings are self-destructive. Instead, I believe we are self-protective, that we're each acting in our best interests—even when it doesn't seem that we are.

Perhaps there's a particular change you've been unable to make. Maybe you want to find someone to love, or you've fallen in love with several people and can't choose one. You may be stuck in a bad relationship, or perhaps you've repeatedly gained and lost the same 5, 20, or 50 pounds. You may hate your job and yet be afraid to quit, or you may know that you're intelligent and creative but still can't figure out what to do with your life.

All of these problems can stubbornly resist your best efforts to solve them. The premise of *When You Can You Will* is that if you have such a problem—one that persists despite your best efforts to solve it—you're not self-destructive or lazy or cowardly or crazy. On the contrary, you're self-protective and self-caring,

1

and you have a *very good reason* for not making this change even if you don't consciously know what that reason is.

OUR INSTANT-SOUP SOCIETY

It's difficult to focus on your reasons for not doing something when you live in a society where you're constantly bombarded by messages urging you to "do it all and do it now!" An old saying that I learned as a child seems even more timely today: "Good, better, best, never let it rest, until your good is better and your better is the best." The pressure is on. Everywhere you look you're encouraged to do more, be more, have more, and achieve more.

Athletic shoe companies lead the way—Reebok warns that "life is short" so we'd better "play hard." Nike enigmatically orders us to "just do it"—to the accompaniment of extraordinary athletes who flash on our TV screens doing things that we ordinary humans couldn't possibly do. Bookstores bulge with books advising us to "feel the fear and do it anyway" or take "the road less traveled." Even the army wants you to "be all that you can be"—at whatever expense to your well-being and happiness.

The advertising industry thrives on "quick fix" solutions. Commercials assure us that loneliness and unhappiness can be cured by drinking this beer or using that toothpaste. We've all seen the commercial for a time-release cold medicine that promises to "keep you going, when you can't keep going."

It hardly seems necessary to point out that if you *can't* keep going, you *shouldn't* keep going. But in a culture that willingly denies this fact in order to sell products, it's important to recognize that there are times when a person just can't keep going. There are times when—for the sake of your overall physical or mental health—it is best to slow down or stop altogether.

At moments like this, when stopping is essential, forcing yourself to continue can actually be harmful. How many of us, with the help of the pharmaceutical industry, have successfully ignored the messages from our bodies and "kept going," only to suffer relapse after relapse of the same flu bug or shin splint?

The physical fitness movement, with its "no pain, no gain" philosophy, is another advocate for "do it all and do it all now!" It insists that sweating, stepping, running, pumping, and the thinness that is supposed to result, will make you desirable. But whoever created the saying "You can never be too thin" was mistaken. They failed to consider the growing number of people who suffer from diseases like anorexia and bulimia, diseases that result from trying to make the human body do something it can't do—be too thin—and that have tragically cost many lives.

No matter how much you want to be loved, admired, rich, or thin, trying to beat yourself into shape won't work. No matter how much you want to—*you can't do what you can't do!*

The remarkable growth of personal technology is another major contributor to the "do it all and do it now" pressure of our world. We have fast food, push-button phones, personal computers, and home delivery of just about anything. Technology is omnipresent, affecting and redefining every aspect of our lives.

Cooking with stove and oven has given way to frozen dinners, packaged instant foods, and the microwave. Dial telephones have become digital, with call waiting, forwarding, and conferencing. Many real live secretaries have been replaced by voice mail. Hobbies and family games long ago lost out to TV and video games. The VCR brings us immediate entertainment—via remote control. Phones, games, computers, and fax machines are everywhere—in the car, briefcase, or pocket—providing us with instant results, instant gratification. Waiting has become obsolete.

The message—however unintentional—is that if everything else can be speeded up, so can we. But there's no shortcut to human change. No matter how quickly society moves, human beings still have to be ready before they can make certain changes.

The idea that we can change ourselves the way we change channels is certainly attractive. If a car or a deodorant can instantly make us more desirable or more competitive, surely we can just as quickly transform ourselves in any number of other ways. Have you inadvertently fallen for the "do it all and do it now" doctrine? Are you measuring yourself against a media standard? Are you using outside indicators to determine if you're "okay"? If so, you may be disregarding important messages coming from your psyche and/or your body and trying to force yourself to do something you can't do at this time.

If you've repeatedly failed to make a change, one you're really sure you want to make, your first reaction may be to tell yourself that you should try harder. "If at first you don't succeed, try, try again." As in the childhood game of hide-and-seek, you may be telling yourself "ready or not, I will change"; but no matter what wonders technology can accomplish, *you* personally have to be ready before you personally can change.

It is undeniably true that continuing effort will often bring success. But when all of your best efforts have failed, you may be up against something you don't recognize: there may be a barrier between you and the change you want to make. When you recognize the existence of this barrier, you may be tempted to accuse yourself of self-sabotage. But for a moment consider the possibility that this barrier is in actuality a protection and that you have a good reason for avoiding this change.

IF YOU CAN'T, YOU MUST!

This saying expresses the currently popular belief that the harder a thing is to do, the harder you must try to do it—with the concomitant belief that if you fail, there's something wrong with you. This simply isn't true!

There will always be difficult or unpleasant things to do in life, but the difficulty of a thing—in and of itself—*does not guarantee growth*. You don't get points or make progress for needlessly enduring pain or suffering. In fact, if a task is too difficult and you fail, you not only won't grow or stretch, but you may actually shrink in self-defense.

Ironically, belief in the maxim "if you can't, you must" sets a person up for failure. You simply can't do what you can't do, and while you're trying to do what you can't do, you're likely to do nothing at all. Attempting to force yourself to do something you can't only leads to failure. That failure lowers self-esteem, and with low self-esteem even the smallest requirements of everyday life are more difficult to fulfill.

Is it hard for you to accept that you're doing the best you can? Do you measure the value of a task by its difficulty? If a particular task scares, repels, or upsets you, do you approve of tackling it? Do you condemn yourself for doing only what you can do and approve of or congratulate yourself for attempting to do what you can't?

When you can't master one of life's difficulties do you accuse yourself of being lazy, weak, stupid, inadequate, stubborn, or self-destructive? This type of self-criticism will only work against you. It creates a vicious circle: first you don't change; then you scold yourself; then you feel bad; then you can't do anything; then you don't change.

Let's say you want to break up with your lover. Perhaps you've even managed to leave, but then had to apologize and return. Seeing that you couldn't do what you wanted to do may have made you angry at yourself, and caused you to call yourself names such as weak, stupid, or self-destructive. The worse the criticism, the worse you feel about yourself. Thinking that you're stupid or self-destructive is depressing and makes you feel hopeless. Obviously, if you feel hopeless it's even more difficult to think about leaving your lover.

So, if wanting, trying, and self-criticizing won't work, what should you do? First, stop for a moment and see if you can shift your attention away from the change and how badly you want to make it. Then, consider the possibility that there may be a good reason that you can't make this change at this time and that by not changing you are actually protecting yourself. Now, begin to wonder what your good reason for *not* changing might be. Ask yourself what you might be protecting yourself from. For example, you may need to stay with a lover you're sure you want to leave to protect yourself from loneliness, other people's pity, poverty, or feeling like a failure.

I'm not suggesting that you shouldn't try to change. Some changes will be easy to make and others, while difficult, will still be possible and well worth the effort they demand. I am suggesting that personal change cannot always be accomplished as easily as advertising and self-help slogans, child-rearing clichés, or childhood games would have us believe. I'm saying that the difficult changes, those stubborn ones that defy your best efforts, shouldn't be treated as simply foolish or annoying obstacles to be gotten around. They must be taken seriously. They must be respected. I'm saying that the difficulty you have making these changes cannot be trivialized, speeded up, or ignored; that this difficulty is a neon stop sign, which must be honored.

When You Can You Will suggests that you look at yourself and your life, from what may, for you, be a new perspective. It encourages you to use the change you can't make as a vehicle to discover yourself. It is my hope that as you understand more about who you are, and specifically, why you can't make the change you want to make, you will appreciate the self-protective aspect of your nature, forgive yourself for not changing, shift your attention from the things you can't do to the things you can do, and enjoy the pleasure and success this is bound to bring you. I begin by cataloging the kinds of obstacles that can block your path to change, starting with those you acquired in childhood.

BACK TO THE FAMILY

Primary among the obstacles that stand firmly between us and the changes we want to make are the beliefs we acquired about ourselves and the world in our early life. Many of the reasons you have for not changing today actually originated in your family. In chapter 2, "It's All in the Family," I explain how families operate, how they teach us—directly and indirectly—who to be and who not to be. I introduce the concept of family balance, the intricate weaving of family roles that is necessary to maintain the family's stability. I demonstrate how, through modeling and antimodeling, we learn which roles to play and which to avoid. And, based on these roles, how we create binding "relationship contracts" with our family members—a concept you can better understand when you have constructed your "family pie."

In chapter 3, "Cover Story," I explain how we create a "cover story," an incomplete picture of ourselves, which we nonetheless believe to be true and present to the world. This story is made up of qualities we admit to having—our "cover"— and qualities we deny having—which go "under cover." In chapter 3, you'll discover that your "hidden" qualities may be the very ones you need in order to make your desired change; how making this change may depend on renouncing your cover and reclaiming your under cover; and why this process can be frightening.

CHANGE IS DANGEROUS

Many of the reasons we have for resisting change are related to danger and fear. Our society is scornful of danger and mocks fear, so it may never have occurred to you to wonder if there's a danger attached to the change you can't make. This fear of danger is natural and appropriate. The "if you can't, you must" school of change dismisses fear, but fear is a signal. When you're afraid, there's usually something quite real to be afraid of. By not changing you may be avoiding something that frightens you. That isn't cowardly—it's prudent.

Chapter 4, "Change Is Dangerous," explores the dangers— "catastrophic expectations"—that might be keeping you from changing. There are "future dangers," encountered when the change you want to make requires you to do something you've never done before, something whose consequences you can't anticipate. There are "past dangers," which appear when the desired change requires you to redo something from your past, something that had unpleasant or even traumatic consequences when you last attempted it.

You may not realize that you have an ally in your struggle to confront the danger you'll face when making the difficult changes. This ally is your unconscious mind.

CONSCIOUS VS. UNCONSCIOUS

Chapters 5 and 6, "Your Unconscious—A Friend in Need" and "Camouflage—The Ultimate Weapon of Your Unconscious," introduce the concept of a user-friendly unconscious. These chapters explain the difference between your conscious and unconscious minds. They demonstrate how each operates in your life, and how each participates in the changes you want to make.

These two chapters illustrate how your unconscious protects you from danger by keeping you from changing prematurely. Chapter 5 describes how, for example, your unconscious uses Freudian slips, helps you make convenient mistakes, and causes you to forget to remember. Chapter 6 illustrates how your unconscious uses "camouflage" to distract you from dangerous changes, how it joins with your body and instructs you through dreams. Together, chapters 5 and 6 demonstrate that you're not restricted to the resources of your conscious mind but have more assets at your disposal than you may have previously believed.

CHANGES IN STAGES

One of the reasons that change seems so difficult to achieve is that it must often occur in stages. Human change is evolutionary, and evolution takes time. You may have to try on the change several times, before you're accustomed to the way it feels, much as you would with a new pair of shoes. One day you can't do the thing you want to do, the next day you can, then the next day you can't do it again, and so on, until one day it fits, it feels right—you've changed. If you don't recognize that this roller coaster ride is a natural process, indeed an indicator of change, you may imagine that you're out of control and feel frightened or discouraged. Recognizing the true nature of change can make the experience more pleasant.

THE THINGS WE DO
FOR CHANGE

Chapter 7, "The Things We Do for Change," discusses the cultural pressure we all feel to be "normal." It enumerates the most popular methods we use when trying to effect change, such as self-knowledge, self-discipline, self-criticism, keeping our eye on the ball, and the all-purpose, one-size-fits-all solution to problems. It explains that while there is no shortage of "sure-fire" techniques to try, none of these tricks and ploys will make you change until you can confront and survive the danger that will accompany the change—in other words, until you're ready.

GETTING READY

Chapter 8, "Readiness—There's No Getting Around It," reminds you that wanting and trying are not enough. It explains that thinking you're ready doesn't mean that you are, and that while believing you can force yourself to do right, be good, get thin, or stay sober may make you feel better, it won't make you able to change. It demonstrates that when you are ready, *you will change*, and you don't even have to know that you're ready because your unconscious will know that you are and help you change either the "easy way" or the "hard way."

Changes made in the easy way are effortless. Suddenly things that seemed impossible are possible. If you've never been able, for example, to express anger, you may one day hear yourself chewing out someone who has treated you badly, and no one will be more surprised than you. When you change the easy way, you often find yourself thinking, saying, and doing things that would have been unthinkable even the day before.

Changes made in the hard way can be difficult, unpleasant, and even frightening. Changes must be made the hard way when, although you are ready to make them, your conscious mind disapproves, or is still too afraid to risk them. When you change the hard way, it can seem as though you're breaking down or falling apart; you may experience the sensation of having your *hand in the flame* or *the fear that feels like dying*. But what appears to be disintegration is actually expansion and will lead to the change you need to make. When you're ready you will change, but making the change isn't the end of the story. Not only is there unanticipated danger behind the change you want to make, but there may also be an unanticipated "price" you have to pay for the change once you've made it.

THE PRICE IS WRONG

Chapter 9, "The Price and the Payoff," outlines three of the most common prices that must be paid for changes achieved. There's the price of the unachieved "secondary payoff," where you receive your primary goal but not a secondary goal, one you didn't even know existed and was even more important than the primary goal you were pursuing. There's the price of breaking a relationship contract, which occurs when the change alters you in a way that makes you no longer fit in some old relationships. Finally, you may have to pay the price of "giving up the dream," the belief—held by many—that someone other than yourself will be the one who takes care of you.

"YOU JUST CAN'T TEACH AN OLD DOG NEW TRICKS!" Until now, you may have explained your inability to change by repeating the old chestnut that "people just don't change." This is another popular cultural misbelief. *Of course people do change!* Sometimes they change very quickly and dramatically. We all know such people: men and women, who after years of loneliness, have married happily; or alcoholics who have become clean and sober. But even when you've already made some pretty significant changes in your own life, if you can't make the change you want to make *today*, you may tell yourself it's because people just don't change.

One of the many gifts of the unconscious is the ability to forget. Human beings have an enormous capacity to forget, not only the pain or hurt of the past, but what we had for lunch. When you've made a lasting change in your life, when you no longer have to struggle to keep a change in place—you've integrated it. When you've thoroughly integrated a change into your self-concept, you frequently forget that you were ever any other way. As a therapist I often wish for an instant replay screen in my office so, when someone complains that "nothing ever changes," or "I'm exactly where I always was," I could show

11

them the place from which they've so recently come. When I describe the way they used to be, people sometimes smile and say that while my description sounds familiar, they no longer feel like that person.

These changes, the ones that become so much a part of your self-concept that you forget you were ever any other way, can't be stuck on. They must evolve naturally.

CHANGE IS AN INSIDE JOB. Before you can make your desired change, you may need to move to a new developmental stage. You may need to change inside before you can change outside. External change is visible, but the internal change that precedes it doesn't show. Consequently, what we learn about how people change from watching others change can be misleading. Changes made by others can seem to come out of the blue. What actually happens is that the change occurs first inside the individual, and we usually see only the external results, not the internal process.

Although this inside job can't be observed, some of us try to control or monitor our progress by dutifully following the dictates of a self-help book or other instruction. But focusing too closely on your problem can actually get in your way. The trouble with "trying" is that it often just means reapplying a solution that's already failed. New solutions to your problem may be necessary, and while you're focusing on an old solution, you may not recognize a new one. Shifting your attention away from the problem can allow you to receive information from other sources, like your unconscious mind or your body. Happily, change often happens when you're not expecting or even thinking about it. We've all had the experience of trying to remember a name, a book title, or a song lyric. We say, "Oh well, it'll come to me later," and it does. It's the same with some changes: sometimes it's necessary to stop trying, and trust that it will come to you later.

When you've read this book; when you understand more about the influence your family had on your life; when you recognize the danger inherent in the change you want to make; when you're on friendly terms with your unconscious and have given up trying to trick yourself into change; when you're aware of the price you may have to pay for your success; if, after all this, you're *still* not changing—then you're *still* not ready. In chapter 10, "In the Meanwhile," I will suggest what to do if you discover yourself in this situation.

ALL YOU NEED IS LOVE. When people come to see me they're often sad, frustrated, and frightened. They're mad at or disappointed in themselves. They want to like themselves but they believe that they must change before this is possible. They come to me hoping that I will make them change. "Be tough on me," they say. "Don't let me get away with anything."

I have to tell them that they have it backwards. *It isn't changing that will make you like yourself—it's liking yourself that will help you change.* It is those of us who feel loved who can risk change—not those of us who are always trying to measure up. The best thing you can do to encourage yourself to be ready to change is to start loving yourself now, flaws and all. The ability to love yourself is the primary requirement of readiness.

Loving yourself is easier said than done. If, like many, you came out of childhood feeling unloved or inadequate, you may find it hard to like, much less love, yourself. You may not know how. Scolding and self-criticism may feel right to you while acceptance or support make you uncomfortable or embarrass you.

If, for the moment, the idea of being the one who loves you is just too difficult or scary, take a break. You may not be able to make the change you want to make until you can begin to love yourself, but don't despair. There is something helpful you can do in the meanwhile: You can have fun.

JUST BECAUSE IT FEELS GOOD. It's difficult to overemphasize the curative powers of pleasure, joy, delight, and plain old garden-variety happiness. When you're happy you feel deserving, and this is your most powerful advocate for change. Unfortunately many people feel helpless if they aren't constantly focusing on their problem. For some, enjoying themselves rather than trying harder feels like rewarding failure. So, many of us occupy ourselves with unproductive busy work rather than taking time off to play.

You may think that you have many good reasons for not enjoying yourself. You may tell yourself that the very minute you accomplish your change you'll make up for all this lost time. But an uncompromising schedule, one that doesn't include joy and pleasure, can have a demoralizing effect; rather than help you change, it can actually get in your way. If wanting and trying haven't made you able to change, if it's too frightening to give yourself the love you want and need, rigorously pursuing the change or mercilessly criticizing yourself for not succeeding, won't help you accomplish your goal.

When you're stuck, the best thing you can do is have some fun. See a movie, get a massage, take a bubble bath, make love, play ball, even watch TV. Pleasure makes you feel good. When you feel good, you like yourself better. When you like yourself better you're more able to take the risks that changing requires.

Perhaps you're thinking "How self-indulgent! How wasteful!" Not so! When you shift your attention away from the "problem," you give yourself an opportunity to be creative and find new solutions. Rod Serling, creator of "The Twilight Zone," said that when he suffered from writer's block, instead of buckling down and trying harder, he found that he could solve his creative problems by taking his mind off them, for example by going to a museum or listening to his favorite symphonic music.

The speed at which you solve a problem or make a change is not directly related to the amount of time or energy you spend working on or worrying about it.

WHEN YOU CAN YOU WILL

People really do change, not always when they want to or wish they would, but when they're ready. Surprisingly, it's often after the fact that you notice you've changed. You catch yourself in the act of the new behavior and in wonder say to yourself, "Who did that? Who said that? It couldn't be me, I can't do that!" The change was so natural, you barely recognized that you were in the midst of it.

I know that this contradicts what many of you believe. I know that some of you may be thinking, "I bought this book to find out how to do what I can't do, not to hear that I should do nothing." I know that you're used to hearing "No pain, no gain," and that if something is "good for you," you should make yourself do it.

But I'm not saying "Don't change," "Don't try," or "Don't do." I'm saying that there are times when you just can't "push the river" and that trying to "push the river" may only lead to failure, self-criticism, disappointment, and pain with no gain.

By all means, do everything you *can* do, but if there's a change you desperately want to make—anything from writing a letter to quitting your job—and, try as you might, you've been unable to make it, maybe you're just not ready.

Changes you're not ready to make cannot be made

- no matter how much you want to make them;
- no matter how hard you try to make them;
- no matter how much believe you should make them; and
- no matter how much others wish you would make them.

When you're ready, you'll change; making yourself miserable in the meantime won't hurry the process. However, even when you can't "push the river" there are still things you can do to encourage change. You can

- learn more about your family;
- expose your cover story;
- discover the danger you're avoiding by not changing;
- spot the silent hand of your unconscious at work in your life;
- encourage readiness by loving yourself;
- prepare for the price you'll have to pay when you do change;

and if change doesn't happen as quickly as you'd like, you can still have a good time.

The cultural belief that people should be able to change whenever they want to is pervasive. Consequently, people who come to see me are often startled when I first tell them that they *can't do what they can't do* and *when they can they will.* "I want to believe you," they may say, "but can it be that easy?"

While we're working in therapy on discovering and addressing the obstacles that block their way to change, the culture (their friends, family, the media) is continually telling them to *just do it!* To counter this pressure I find that I often have to repeat what I know to be true. Just as I do it within a therapy session, I do it in this book, repeat over and over again, that it may seem paradoxical and contrary to what you've always heard, but you can't do what you can't do, and When You Can You Will.

It's All in
the Family

———

Our family and the earliest years of our childhood are the most significant factors determining who we become and what we can and can't do in our lives. It is the job of the family to instruct us and, intentionally or unintentionally, that is just what it does. Those early lessons, many of which we learned before we had the words with which to articulate them, wield a powerful influence over us for the rest of our lives.

It may be a cliché, but it's nonetheless true that what you believe you can and can't do today is based primarily on lessons you learned within your family. Your family was the laboratory where you conducted your most important research. It was there that you learned

- who you had to be;
- who you'd better not be;
- what to expect from the world; and
- what the world expected of you.

Ignoring the legacy of your childhood won't make it go away. You may never act on the information you learn here, but the more you know about the lessons you were taught by your family, the better you'll understand your reluctance to make meaningful changes today.

You may believe that you've left behind whatever influence your family once had over you. You may not like or even speak to your family members today. But events you've forgotten, ideas you've outgrown, attitudes you believe you've discredited, and alliances you deny still reach out from the past to affect your idea of who you are. And this idea of yourself determines how smoothly you can operate in the world.

Your idea of who you are is based, not on who you actually are, but on how you interpreted the needs of your family:

- your place in the birth order;
- your sex;
- who you were named for;
- who you look like;
- who the family needed a child to be when you were born;
- who your parents were; and
- how you modeled yourself after them.

Criteria like these formed the basis for your idea of yourself. By carefully observing what worked and what didn't work in your particular family you decided which parts of your personality to express and which to hide. Your decision to present certain qualities and hide others was based on how well each quality was received by your family. Responding positively or negatively, family members let you know, often instantly, which of your behaviors were acceptable and which taboo. Self-protectively, over time, you displayed one and disowned another. The more your parents accepted you as you really were, the less you had to invent or hide. The less you were their idea of the perfect child, the more you had to create or deny. If the change you want to make today requires you to be someone you weren't allowed to be as a child, you may face strong internal resistance to that change. If the change you want to make today requires you to express a quality that was unacceptable to your family when you were a child, you may, as an adult, still feel a taboo against expressing that quality. If, for example, your mother believed that men were brash and women shy, she communicated this belief to you. As her son, you found it easy to speak your mind; as her daughter, you didn't.

Let's say you are this daughter and the change you want to make today is to stand up for yourself in your marriage. In your mind's eye, you can still see your mother's scowling face and feel her disapproval of an outspoken daughter. This alone can make it difficult to do what *you* want to do. You may not actually remember your mother's scowling face. You may think that you're no longer affected by what your mother believed or what she taught you. But roles adopted in childhood are such well-worn reflexes that, even if you don't see that subliminal flash of your mother's disapproving face, it still affects you.

The idea that events from the past can influence your ability to make decisions in the present may annoy you. You may even want to discount this possibility altogether. But as the philosopher George Santayana wrote, "those who cannot remember the past are condemned to repeat it." The more you know about the legacy of your childhood, the better you grasp the lessons your family taught you, the more clearly you understand who they taught you to be and what they taught you to expect from life, the better chance you will have to circumvent whatever "stop" messages they gave you and replace them with "go" messages of your own.

FAMILIES—A PRECARIOUS BALANCE

Families are not random, haphazard, or accidental collections of individuals. They're made up of a series of very carefully and delicately balanced alliances. They are, to use the technical term, homeostatic. This term, borrowed by psychology from physics, is defined by Webster as "a state of . . . equilibrium produced by a balance of functions." Checks and balances, like those prescribed by the U.S. Constitution to balance the executive, legislative, and judicial branches of our federal government, actually do operate within our families.

If you look carefully at your own family, you may begin to see how it is balanced, to notice repeated patterns of behavior. Think about the casual descriptions of your family members. The men may be loud, hardworking, or aloof; the women caretaking, sensitive, or sneaky; the parents may be hippies and the children yuppies or vice versa; the girls genteel and the boys crude; the whole family may be careful except for one child who is a daredevil. Whatever the division, there will probably be some kind of balance.

In fact, families are so carefully balanced that if any member changes—say, if the hippie gets a job, or the yuppie goes on welfare—the balance of the entire family shifts and everyone is suddenly in danger of losing their equilibrium. Once you've accepted a role, the balance of your family depends on your maintaining it. Consequently, if the change you want to make means giving up your "assigned" role in the family, your family's dependence on you to play that role will affect your ability to make the change. The unconscious unwillingness to upset family balance is often a major obstacle to change.

ALL THE FAMILY QUALITIES EXIST IN ALL THE FAMILY MEMBERS

The qualities that exist within families are like intelligence agency operations—some are overt and some are covert. I know that this statement may contradict what you believe to be true. You may believe that you "are the way you are" and that your family members are also just "the way they are." You may believe that both you and your family members *are* the roles you've all been playing. But it's not true. It's much more likely that each of you has been denying aspects of yourself for the sake of the family's balance. Not only you, but all of your family members, are capable of being very different people, but your natural reluctance to unbalance the rest of the family stops each of you from changing.

If you envy a quality possessed by another family member, you may believe that you'll have to struggle to achieve it, or even that it is impossible for you to achieve. *It is possible for you to achieve this quality—in fact, it may already be part of your makeup*. But in order to protect yourself and your family's balance you have thus far denied it.

Ask yourself how different your life would be if you suddenly possessed this denied quality. What would be the effect of this change on your family's balance? Suppose you were no longer timid, but were suddenly outspoken? What if you were no longer irresponsible, but dependable? How would the members of your family act toward you if you were no longer poor, but suddenly made a lot of money?

Since these are qualities you'd like to change about yourself, your first answers are likely to represent the upside: You'd be happy, employed, loved, rich. Your family would be pleased, relieved, delighted, surprised. After you've examined all the benefits of this change, look for the downside, the danger or the unpleasant side effects that might accompany the switch. What new and scary things might be expected of you? Who would be surprised, shocked, or astonished? Who would be scared, angry, disappointed, or jealous? Who would be threatened, left holding the bag, or out of a job?

We rarely ask ourselves these kinds of questions, and for good reason. It's upsetting to think that a change that would enhance our life could upset our whole family's balance. We much prefer to think of ourselves as free agents, unattached to and unencumbered by the needs and expectations of our loved ones. But we are delicately bound by invisible threads. These threads can be severed, but you have to know where they are before you can attempt the surgery.

EXERCISE—*The "Family Pie"*

The purpose of this exercise is to begin to highlight some of the threads by which you are bound to your family. The better you understand the roles that were assigned in your family—especially the role *you* are expected to play—the better you'll be able to differentiate between your role and your true self. This exercise can help you begin the discovery-recovery process that will, in turn, prepare you to change.

First, get a large piece of blank paper and two different-colored pens. Choose one color to represent you. Draw a big circle and divide it into as many pieces as there were people in your original family. Label each one of the pieces with the name of a family member, including yourself.

Then, in each segment of the pie, write a detailed list of the qualities that describe the person named there. Write the qualities that describe you in one color (say, green) and everyone else's qualities in the other color (black, perhaps). Whenever your qualities—the ones you've written in your pie piece—show up in someone else's pie piece, write them in your color, green.

Take your time doing this. Think carefully about each person as you describe them. Some family members will be very easy to describe. Others may, for now, be blank pieces in your family pie.

Consider getting some help in the description process. If possible, enlist your siblings or cousins. You may be surprised at the difference of opinion or amazing agreement among yourselves. It may seem that you had different parents. Their description of you, or of themselves, might startle you. Or, as is most often the case, you may find that you all basically agree about who everyone is, and what everyone's role in the family has been. This information is not only interesting but useful as you begin the recovery process.

DIGESTING THE PIE

The first thing to recognize is that the qualities you have used to describe yourself—the ones in your pie piece—are the qualities that make up your *idea* of who you are, the ones assigned by your family, to maintain its balance. But while true of you, these qualities are only a *part* of who you really are.

Perhaps you described yourself as insecure or irresponsible. If you've written "secure" or "responsible" in someone else's pie piece, these qualities may be yours as well.

Take some time to wonder why you adopted these particular qualities, how you learned to be who you are:

- What messages about yourself did you receive as a child?
- What stories about you are still being told?
- What was your nickname?
- Are you the one who was "always late for school"?
- Were you the one "Mommy could always count on"?
- Were you the "little angel" or the "little devil"?

If you look carefully at your history, you may be able to see how you were guided or encouraged to act in a particular way, or to think of yourself as a particular kind of person. You may approve or disapprove of the part you were cast to play in your family drama, but this is the person you decided your family needed you to be.

23

Families frequently contain stark contrasts: one child will be neat and one sloppy, one studious and another athletic. In this way balance is maintained but often at the expense of the full development of any of the children. Let's say that your older brother was designated as the caring one while you were cast as the callous one. If you look back on your childhood, you may see how you were discouraged, albeit subtly, from expressing your ability to care, while your brother was equally inhibited from the natural expression of childish callousness or un-concern.

In their zeal to achieve balance families can turn po-tentially fully developed and well-rounded children into polarized, one-dimensional adults. To find the qualities you possess but have been denying, look at the pie pieces of your other family members. The qualities you've written there may also belong to you, but you've kept them a secret even from yourself.

Some of these may be qualities that you've always wished you had. You may, for example, have always envied your sister's neatness or your mother's ability to entertain. There may also be qualities you're glad you were spared, like your father's temper or your brother's recklessness. Ironically, these qualities that you have, up to now, rejected may be the very ones you need to make the change you want to make. But as you embark on the discovery-recovery process, remember that you had a very good reason for keeping these traits hidden.

THE "GREAT TRAIT SWAP"

When family members relinquish a role they've always played, they leave a void. Since family balance requires that all roles continue to be played, someone else must then assume the abandoned role. If, for example, little sister is no longer willing to be the family scapegoat, those whose role it had been to tease or blame her will now have no one to harass. Pressure will then be put on the remaining family members to fill the void—someone else must become the family scapegoat.

As long as you're convinced that people are just "the way they are," you may find it hard to believe that family roles are interchangeable. But it is nonetheless true. If you change the role you've been playing in your family, others will feel pressured to change as well.

Let's say that you've always been the quiet one, and you suddenly become talkative. Then, the stillness, the role of the listener that you abandoned, will hang there waiting to be claimed by someone else. The role of the listener *must* be played by someone—when you start talking, someone else must listen.

Those who have always seen themselves as the talkers are likely to feel anxious when their role is threatened, when they are no longer at center stage. And, however much you want to make this change, when you actually start talking, you're likely to feel anxious at losing your "identity" as the quiet one who could always get lost in the crowd.

Even if you have the capacity to be a very different person, the pressure to continue being who you've always been and allow others to maintain their comfortable roles is enough to keep you in your place. Even if you are all perpetuating a fiction, it's a fiction with a purpose and one that is not easily ignored, exposed, or overturned.

This trait exchange cannot take place until one individual in the family *really changes* his or her role. Acting as if you are, or pretending to be, someone you're not, won't work. You must actually cast off the trait or role. But as soon as you do, there is a magical quality about the way the role you've abandoned is transferred to another family member. Mary's story is a classic and happy example of an ideal trait swap.

Mary, the oldest child in her family, and her father's favorite, always felt responsible for the happiness and well-being of her parents. She didn't like having to worry about them, but assumed that this concern just came with the territory of being a caring person. Her younger sister, Eileen, was considered the selfish one in the family.

Mary was 45 years old when she came to see me. She was suffering from exhaustion and it didn't take long for her to recognize the role she was playing in her family and her life. In therapy Mary worked on developing her ability to take better care of herself and slowly learned to resist the temptation to put the needs of others before her own. After a year she quit her job and gave her surprised husband an ultimatum about sharing the household chores. Mary had clearly changed.

Shortly thereafter, when Mary and Eileen's mother became ill, Mary, who had always been the one to run to the rescue, just didn't "feel like it." Eileen became very worried about their mother's condition. She made a series of frantic calls to Mary, trying to get her to "do her job," but when Mary held firm, Eileen volunteered to help their father care for their mother. Leaping into what had previously been Mary's role, Eileen became the caretaker.

The role of family rescuer and parent to the parent that Mary returned to the pie had to go to someone. In this case the returned role was adopted by someone who'd always wanted it. Both Mary and Eileen were happy—Mary was finally able to give up her role as the family rescuer, and Eileen was finally able to be taken more seriously by her parents.

When you change, somebody else has to change, but we're all attached to, and comfortable with, the roles we know. Still, taking on one quality means giving up another quality, and vice versa. And because we all instinctively know this, not only are we reluctant to make changes that might unbalance the family, but the family is equally reluctant to have us try.

HOW FAMILIES RESIST CHANGE

When another family member is open to the switch, the great trait swap can greatly benefit both people, allowing them to expand their ideas of themselves and increase what they're capable of experiencing. But more often, other family members resist the exchange. Even if they don't actually like their old role, they're identified with it and reject the new role because it is one they have disowned or denied. Even Eileen, who really *wanted* to play the rescuer role in her family, first tried to get Mary to continue in the role before she accepted it. Everyone is more comfortable with the status quo.

Family members may sincerely believe that they *want* you to change. Let's say you've always been the family failure, urged by one and all to succeed. *Until another family member can accept the role you're abandoning* and allow themselves to fail, the family may not be able to afford to have you change. Without realizing it, family members who are unable to participate in the great trait swap may discourage your changing. The entire family can join in subtle and direct attempts to discourage the person who is trying to change. They can actually ignore the change after it's made. Gerri, in the following example, discovered this the hard way.

Acting out her role as the impulsive one in her family, Gerri struggled with a weight problem all of her life. Her thin mother and older sister, who prided themselves on being responsible and in control, constantly teased and chided her. At family gatherings they took turns watching to see that Gerri didn't overeat. When she came to their homes, they hid the sweets.

Gerri came to see me when, at 32 years old, she'd moved to California from her native Oregon. She was suffering from a depression, which made her even more impulsive and, consequently, heavier. In therapy Gerri drew her family pie, and began to wonder if she, too, possessed the qualities of responsibility and self-control she'd always thought of as belonging to her mother and sister.

It was exciting but also frightening for Gerri to think that she might be as "grown-up" as her mother and sister. Over a two-year period Gerri was able to accept these qualities, which

27

she'd denied all of her life, and lost 50 pounds. She returned for a family wedding expecting a celebration of her own. To her amazement, no one in the family even mentioned her weight loss. They continued acting out their old roles of "watching" her and "hiding" food. Gerri had given up her role as the impulsive eater, but her mother and sister were unable to give up their roles as the monitors of Gerri's impulses.

Although Gerri had successfully renounced her impulsive role and was able to maintain her weight loss, she had to give up hoping that her family would recognize and applaud her accomplishment. Their inability to accept their own impulsiveness, or their need to be cared for, forced them to pretend that she was still overweight and needed them to watch her.

The equilibrium of our families is so vital that we all make sacrifices to maintain this delicate balance. Our happiness, success, self-esteem, even our physical well-being can be casualties in this cause.

Jenny came to see me because her sister Lucille was threatening to commit suicide, and Jenny wanted to stop her. In their family everyone except Lucille had a caretaker role. Lucille's role as the incompetent one who had to be protected had guaranteed that the other family members had someone to take care of. At 35, Lucille was tired of being incompetent but she couldn't bear to unbalance the family by exposing her ability to take care of herself. She would literally rather have died first.

If you can't make a change you want to make—even if your family seems to support you in this change—you may, with the unwitting help of your family, be sacrificing yourself for the good of your family's balance. The pressure to remain in your assigned role can be direct, as with Eileen's telephone calls to Mary urging her to "do her job," or they can be very subtle, very difficult to detect. Try the next exercise to help determine if you're holding yourself back from the change you want to make, in order not to upset your family's apple cart.

EXERCISE—*Small Change*

You may think I'm exaggerating and that families couldn't possibly be as rigidly balanced as I suggest, but doing the following exercise may change your mind. Think carefully about the qualities for which you are well known in your family. For example, are you the polite one or the rude one? Choose an insignificant character trait, something that couldn't possibly unbalance an entire family. Perhaps you're the one who always cleans her plate or the one who picks at his food. Maybe you're the snappy dresser in your clan, or it could be you're the sloppy one. Try changing just one little trait. Clean your plate or pick at your food, whichever is the opposite of what you usually do; or change the way you usually dress.

You may notice some resistance within yourself to making even this small alteration. You may even feel some anxiety. If you can ignore this self-generated resistance and make the change anyway, be on the lookout for a reaction from your family. They may tease you, make jokes about you, or ask you if you're okay. If the role you've altered is one that is especially important to the family, there may be more serious expressions of concern and stronger attempts to get you back on track, to bring you back to being *the old you,* to doing it *the old way.*

If you decide to try this exercise, but find that even thinking about making this change brings your anxiety level up too high, pass on it for now. You have your answer: Even the smallest things can be hard to change if they threaten your role in your family.

GETTING TO BE WHO WE ARE

If the family balance requires it, the family can get a clever child to act dumb, or turn a naturally curious child into a

29

disinterested one. As a therapist I often meet brave men who consider themselves cowards and beautiful women who think themselves ugly. Families have many ways of instructing you in the role they need you to play. They encourage you when you play the role right and discourage you when you play it wrong. Parents can be straightforward and direct. They say "Stop that"; "You know I don't like that"; "Don't cry"; "Go back to bed, you know you're not strong"; "What a brave boy you are"; "What a sweet temperament you have"; or simply, "That's my good boy/girl!" They can make their intentions oblique and say, "You're just like your brother," or "If you're not careful you'll end up just like crazy Uncle Joe," or "I always knew you'd turn out like your father." Finally, parents can make their intentions indirectly known through nonverbal communication: smiling, shrugging their shoulders, rolling their eyes, hugging, turning their back, or walking out of the room.

MODELING

One of the most powerful tools at the family's disposal is the natural tendency of children to model, or copy, their parents.

Combined with the messages about who your parents wanted *you* to be are the lessons you learned from observing who *they* were. If your parents were happy with themselves and each other, you probably modeled yourself after the parent of the same sex. Generally speaking this is the best option. When you identify with your same-sex parent, you validate all the things you are. If you're a woman and you want to be "just like Mommy," then your womanness, which is actually "just like Mommy," is confirmed.

While identifying with your same-sex parent is the most positive choice you can make, it can have negative consequences. Children believe that when they model a parent, they must *take on the whole package*. They don't realize they can take some qualities and leave others. This misunderstanding causes them to adopt qualities they don't want. When they want to jettison some of these traits later in life, they may not realize that it's their identification with their parent that's stopping them. Laura, for example, modeled herself after her mother, Clara, a wise and gentle woman whom Laura loved very much. Clara's early life had been spent in poverty; consequently she was cautious and often frightened. Laura, whose life had always been safe and filled with abundance, nonetheless often felt afraid and unexplicably hoarded things she could well afford to replace.

Another negative aspect of identifying with the parent of the same sex is that when you *do* abandon a characteristic you share with a loved parent, it can feel like a betrayal. People who can't stop smoking often have a same-sex parent who is also addicted to cigarettes, and while they rarely recognize it, it is their identification with the parent that keeps them from quitting. Diane hadn't realized that being a smoker was her way of "siding with" her mother. Diane's mother had a younger sister named April, who didn't smoke. April had always been considered the good one in their family and Diane's mother was very jealous of her younger sister. When Diane stopped smoking it was as if she too, like the rest of the family, had "sided with Aunt April." Diane saw her rejection of smoking as a rejection of her mother.

Most of us are consciously or unconsciously reluctant to outdo our parents, especially the same-sex parent. You may dislike them today and deny that they influence your life, but before you had the words with which to think these thoughts, your parents were the complete focus of your life. You wanted to please them, be like them, and keep them happy at all costs. It was then that you vowed not to distress or upset these giants on whom your life depended.

Even today, doing better than your parents did in any way can feel like an indictment of them. After all, if you're happily married, successful in business, have lots of friends, or remain sober, why couldn't they? Frank assured me that in a few

31

months, when he was finally vested, after fifteen years in the company pension plan, he was going to quit and start his own business. It was his lifelong dream, he said. He'd meant to begin a business long ago, but something had always stopped him. Now the day was definitely approaching. He would finally do it.

When I asked if his father had ever owned his own business, Frank laughed and said, "Lots of them."

"He was a good businessman then?" I asked.

"Oh no," replied Frank, "he failed at every one!"

To see if you've identified with your same-sex parent, look at your family pie. If all or many of the qualities you've written in your pie piece are also in the pie piece of your same-sex parent, you've modeled yourself on that parent. If the change you want to make requires you to alter or relinquish a characteristic you share with that parent, you may be stopped from making this change by your belief that you have to *take the whole package* and/or your reluctance to betray the parent, who has not as yet been able to make this change.

Even if you have strongly modeled a parent, you can still make a change for yourself that your parent has never been able to make. The first step toward making that change is to recognize that one of the things stopping you is that you are a loving child trying to protect a cherished parent.

ANTIMODELING

If you disliked or had contempt for your same-sex parent, you may have chosen to disown their characteristics and copy those of your opposite-sex parent. This may be true if you're a woman who says things like, "I'm nothing like my mother," or a man who says, "It really makes me mad when my wife says that I'm just like my dad."

When a same-sex parent is sick or hurtful, when you despise or distrust the same-sex parent, or when the opposite-sex parent is more attractive, or more terrifying, you may choose to identify with your opposite-sex parent. Even with the tiny amount of information at their disposal, children always make the wisest and most self-protective choice, at the time.

When you identify with the opposite-sex parent, however, even though it's the best possible choice at the time, it can cost you a great deal in later life. When you reject your same-sex parent, you reject something essential about yourself. We all instinctively know this, so when you identify with your opposite-sex parent, you may feel out of sync. You may suspect that there is something bad or flawed about you—something you must keep a secret, even from yourself. That *something* is a characteristic you cannot help sharing with your same-sex parent, something you believe is "bad" and have consequently denied even to yourself. Unfortunately, as an adult, you may find it is precisely this despised and disowned quality that you need to make the change you want to make.

Belinda came to see me because she was having panic attacks. In enclosed places she would suddenly have trouble breathing or feel as though she was going to faint.

Belinda described herself as "a self-sufficient woman." She was not at all, she stressed, like her asthmatic mother, who'd been totally dependent on her father. Belinda had always felt sorry for, and been embarrassed by, her mother. She'd identified with her "independent and successful" father. She'd been successful herself. She'd always thought she'd marry but had somehow never found "Mr. Right."

At 33, although she didn't recognize it, Belinda was ready to recover a quality she'd antimodeled or disowned—her ability to trust. Her self-sufficient role had served her well, but it had also cost her dearly. It was her terror of becoming dependent like her mother, not her difficulty finding "Mr. Right," that had kept her from marrying. Before Belinda could marry she had to know that trusting a man would not lead to losing herself.

When Belinda felt her own urge to trust surfacing, it reminded her of her mother and triggered her mother's asthmatic symptoms. In therapy, Belinda began to think differently about her own ability to trust. She began to understand it outside the context of her mother's dependence. She realized that when she allowed herself to experience her ability to trust she didn't have to take on the *total package* of her mother's characteristics, such as her asthma attacks, fearfulness, and total dependence. Belinda's panic attacks stopped as quickly as they had begun, and about six months later Belinda found her "Mr. Right."

Having to accept that you're in some way like a despised or terrifying parent can be a powerful obstacle to change. If, in your family pie, you see that you share no qualities with your same-sex parent, or share many qualities with your opposite-sex parent, you've identified with your opposite-sex parent. This means that you are denying aspects of yourself and the change you want to make may require you to claim these qualities.

LOVE/HATE

If your same-sex parent was someone you loved and admired, you probably modeled yourself after him or her. But if that parent also had qualities you despised, you may be stuck in a difficult double bind until you understand that you don't have to take the whole package. It took Roger many years to realize that he hadn't married because of his fear that he'd be just like his dad.

Roger loved his dad and his dad loved him. They shared many interests and spent a great deal of time together. Roger was treated very well by his father and had no personal reason to be angry at him, or to disown him. But his father was abusive to Roger's mother. He was constantly critical of her and didn't even try to hide the fact that he cheated on her. Roger also loved his mother and felt responsible for her. He had a real dilemma. He identified with Dad, but he didn't want to be the kind of person who hurt Mom.

Roger solved this problem by modeling his father in every way except one: he never married. Without realizing it, Roger feared that if he married, he'd become just like Dad and hurt his wife. Until Roger was 40, this choice hadn't been a problem for him. But when he decided that he really did want to get married, and had difficulty accomplishing it, he finally had to confront his dilemma.

In your family pie, you may find that you share all, or most, of the qualities you've attributed to your same-sex parent. There may, however, be one or two of their traits that you absolutely *don't* want to share.

"TRADITION, TRADITION"

Like hand-me-down clothes, family roles are passed on from generation to generation. An old joke brings home this truth: Steve asked his wife, Julia, why she made pot roast by cutting the meat into two pieces and putting each in a separate pot. Julia said that this was her mother did it. When Mother was asked why she used two pots, she said she learned this technique from her own mother, who had in turn learned it from hers. Finally Great-Grandma Esther was asked to explain the two-pot method. "Well," she said, "I did it because I didn't have a big enough pot to hold the whole piece of meat."

Despite their best efforts, parents are more than likely to pass on to their children exactly what they learned from their families. As the oldest child in her poor family, Gloria grew up feeling responsible and unappreciated. At 21 she married a selfish, uncaring man and began a very unpleasant married life. At 51 she came into therapy so depressed that she was considering suicide. After a year of therapy Gloria was finally able to tell her husband that she wanted a divorce. Gloria's grown children, however, put up a terrible fuss. In a family therapy session, all of the children talked about their childhood experiences. The oldest child, Ellen, described her feelings about herself in exactly the same language Gloria had used to describe hers. She said that she'd always felt "responsible and unappreciated." Gloria began to cry and said, "Oh honey, the last thing I wanted was to do that to you." Gloria had identified with her own overworked and unappreciated mother, just as Ellen had identified with Gloria. Until you recognize that a role is only a role, you will not only continue to act it out, but you will pass it on.

Because family patterns are unquestioningly passed from generation to generation, it can be useful to draw your "extended-family pie," one that represents both your mother and father's families. Use the same family pie method you used to draw your family of origin and see if you can identify patterns that emerge in your extended family. What was your mother's role in *her* family, or your father's role in *his?* Perhaps like Janet in the following example, you'll find that you were assigned a grandparent's role, one that skipped an entire generation.

Janet was confused when she drew her family pie. In her own pie piece she'd described herself as "courageous" and "risk taking," and her life bore out this description. However, none of her other family members had qualities that remotely resembled hers. In fact, she'd always had contempt for the "caution" and "fear" she'd observed in the rest of her family. Where did she get these pioneering qualities? she wondered. Then she drew her extended-family pies. Both sets of her grandparents had emigrated from the countries of their birth, leaving their homes and their families behind to build a life in a new and unknown country. They were, Janet realized, very "risk taking." It seems that Janet's parents, the children of these courageous people, balanced the uncertainty of their parents' lives with the qualities of caution and stability. Perhaps Janet's family had had enough risk taking in one generation and needed a rest; so it wasn't until the next generation that the family felt safe enough to assign another individual the risk-taking role.

Recognizing that her courage was being carefully balanced by the caution of the rest of her family changed the way Janet viewed her other family members. For the first time in her life Janet was able to consider that there might be an advantage to sometimes being cautious. For the first time in her life, she had an opportunity to expand her own role—her idea of who she had to be.

JOINING FORCES

In your attempt to unlearn or expand the role assigned to you by your family, you may have unexpected allies. Other family members can sometimes be your best source of information and assistance as you struggle to reclaim your whole self.

Siblings are often assigned opposite roles. This means that each is unbalanced and that both need the quality the other has. Alan and Steve are brothers who live in different states. While not antagonistic to each other, they weren't very close. They rarely spoke and saw each other only at family functions.

As the older, Alan was the responsible, dependable, caretaking one. At 48, his life consisted of a series of responsibilities: his business, his elderly parents, his current wife and child, his ex-wife and children, his ulcer, his migraines, his colitis. He was referred to me by his physician because his role was killing him.

I encouraged Alan to call his brother, Steve, and talk about the trouble he was having throwing off his responsible role. Alan was reluctant. He'd always thought of Steve as a loser, certainly not someone from whom he could learn anything. But as the good boy he was, Alan made the call. He was amazed to find Steve in a similar predicament: trying to change his role as the dependent one in the family.

As the baby in the family, Steve was considered passive and helpless. At 42 he was in a dead-end job and married for the second time to a caretaking but domineering wife. Having gone into therapy in desperation, Steve had discovered that his role was incapacitating him.

The brothers' parents had needed a child to take care of them—Alan—and one for them to take care of—Steve. For many years both children had felt burdened by their assigned roles and jealous of the other. Steve coveted Alan's good job, competence, and position as the family hero, and Alan envied Steve's ability to let things just roll off his back and be loved by their parents, no matter how badly he performed in life.

Steve needed what Alan had—the ability to do—and Alan needed what Steve had—the ability to let others do. But each one's role had been heavily reinforced by their parents. And even though their parents regularly encouraged Alan to slow down and Steve to speed up, both brothers instinctively knew that their parents wouldn't like it when they changed.

Alan and Steve had a deeply satisfying conversation. They shared information about their childhoods and discovered how each came to adopt his particular role. Over the course of many such conversations they became friends and allies in their struggle to become whole. And when the inevitable resistance came—when their parents complained that Alan stopped visiting and that Steve stopped confiding in them—they called each other to commiserate and gain the strength to hold their ground.

The need of families to polarize encourages a favorite family pastime—gossip. Entire evenings can be spent bemoaning Aunt Sally's flashy life-style or brother Joe's drinking habits. These conversations with other family members may feel good, but they only serve to confirm Aunt Sally and brother Joe's inadequate roles, and the gossiper's caring or critical role. Instead of discussing, criticizing, or trying to change one another, however, you can become an ally with family members. Like Alan and Steve, you can actually help one another achieve change and provide support in the face of family resistance. But this can only be done when, like Alan and Steve, both people are able to change, to make the great trait swap.

Roles you've been playing for a lifetime are stubborn and persistent. Changing them means contradicting yourself. Suppose the change you want to make is to stand up for yourself, but all of your life you believed that standing up for yourself is an obnoxious trait that would only get you in trouble. If you have a lifetime of experience being a passive person, you know all there is to know about being a passive person and nothing about being an assertive one. You don't know how you will feel, what to expect in return, how others will react, or even how you will react.

New life roles don't come with instructions; there are no job descriptions. New life roles are all learned on the job. Consequently, they're never performed smoothly at the beginning. You must often make mistakes, be awkward, and do it wrong before you can really do it right.

Changing the way you *are*, your idea of yourself, the role you play in the world, is the most difficult habit to break. If the change you want to make requires you to change an aspect of who you are, just the weight of the habit can be enough to stop you. Also, such changes usually require a trait swap with one or more of your family members. To do this you must believe that you *can* be more than "who you are." You must question the merit of the trait you're giving up, value the trait you're taking on, and be willing to unbalance your family.

STAYING PUT

It was your family who taught you the roles you play in life. It was within your family that you forged your idea of who to be and who not to be. It was your family's need for balance that determined your choice of roles and it is their continuing need that still binds you to those roles. But that's not all that's stopping you from change. There are also conditions in your present life that may likewise be effectively blocking your path to change.

In addition to your birth family, there are now probably many other people in your life whom you've trained to expect you to be the person you've always been. Without realizing it we instinctively duplicate the relationships we had with our family. Our friends, lovers, spouses, children, neighbors, and employers become stand-ins for family members. We choose people who expect to be treated—pleased, protected, or abused—in just the way our family members needed to be treated. This guarantees that there are always plenty of people in our lives who will be upset if we abandon our role.

Your spouse and children, close circle of friends, employer, employees, and colleagues make up your current family with whom you today establish balance. You may be out of touch with your original family, but you can't renounce your own need for balance. As long as you believe that you can only play the role you played in your family, you need others to play the roles you denied or disowned. The roles once played by your family members must now be played by others.

LOVE IS A MANY-BALANCED THING

This is especially true for spouses and lovers. You may think you're looking for someone who is generous, good-looking, rich, or intelligent, when you're really seeking someone to balance your role with theirs.

The qualities we had to deny as children but need in order to become whole are the qualities we find irresistible in others. It is this need to create balance that draws us to one another. You probably realize that your choice of partner or mate wasn't random or accidental, but you may not realize that this choice was based on your need to supply yourself with qualities you're missing.

This is why we so often find a spendthrift with a penny-pincher, a gadabout with a stay-at-home, a party animal with a recluse, a religious zealot with an atheist, one with a short fuse with one who never gets angry, a coward with a daredevil, or— as Stephen Sondheim put it in "Send in the Clowns"—"one who keeps tearing around" with "one who can't move." Unfortunately, as long as you still think of the qualities you had to deny as *bad*, you can't appreciate them in others either. Consequently, you often hear people admitting quizzically that the very quality that once attracted them to their lover is the one they now want to change.

KNOWING CHANGE WHEN YOU SEE IT

It is the response of your families—original and current—that is the litmus test that validates your change. You may not see just how delicately balanced your family is until you actually begin to change, but when other family members begin to feel unbalanced you will know for certain that you're changing. A sure sign that this is happening is when you begin to hear questions or statements like one or more of the following:

"Are you sure you're okay?"

"Do you know what you're doing?"

"What's going on?"

"You're disappointing us."

"You're hurting us."

"You're letting us down."

These queries can come directly from close family members like a spouse, parents, or children. They can come from extended-family members like cousins, aunts, or grandparents. Nonfamily members can also be called upon to apply pressure.

41

You may hear from your wife's best friend, or your husband's boss.

When 58-year-old Theresa stopped spending every weekend with her elderly parents, she got a reproachful call from their next-door neighbors, who just wanted her to know how much her parents missed her and looked forward to her next visit.

You may not have anticipated or be prepared for the reaction you get, but if you really begin to make a significant change in who you are, there will more than likely be a reaction from those people who have counted on your being the way you have always been.

THE RELATIONSHIP CONTRACT

In all relationships, beginning with the relationships between family members, there is an unwritten, usually unacknowledged contract which states that each person will continue to be who they were when the relationship began, to play their accepted role. Once we know that someone else is playing a particular role—that he or she is the smart one, the aggressive one, the saver, or the initiator—we can stop worrying about that aspect of life, and focus on playing our role. This contract clarifies relationships, but there is a price for it.

When you try to change, you may not realize that you're bound by this contract. Loved ones may seem to be encouraging the change, but the pressure not to break the contract is powerful.

The change you want to make may require you to stop playing your role and break the contract. The longer the other person has counted on the *old* you, the harder it'll be for them to accept the *new* you. Your change may mean that a role which was once played *for* them may now have to be played *by* them, and they may not be ready to accept that role. For this reason other people, *especially* your loved ones, may not be able to support your change and may even work against it.

Relationship contracts, because they stipulate that you'll always be who you've always been, can be a major obstacle to change. If you believe that your happiness or your survival depends on the support of your loved ones, you may not be able to bear their disappointment or disapproval. If this is true for you, you may not be able to make the change that exposes you to their rejection.

It's easy to deny the effect your family had on you. It's comforting to pretend that you're a free agent, bound to no one but yourself. It's pleasing to think that you're no longer affected by what your family thought about you or what they taught you about yourself and the world. It may be easy, comforting, and pleasing—but it's not true.

Think about the patterns that exist in your family. Ask yourself what role you played in your family drama. Consider if the change you want to make will upset the balance that once existed in your original family or now exists in your current one. Ask yourself if your inability to change could in any way be connected to your need to protect yourself or your family.

In order to make certain changes it may be necessary for you to reclaim your disowned qualities. In chapter 3, "Cover Story," I'll describe at length how to differentiate between those qualities you accept and present—what I term your "cover"—and those you deny and hide—your "under cover"—and describe how to reclaim and appreciate your denied self.

Cover Story

———

To achieve and maintain their balance, families carefully teach each child the role he or she must play. That role, which is essential to the smooth functioning of the family, becomes your "cover story." In the following pages you will see how you created your cover story and how your reluctance to "blow your cover" can stop you from changing.

Everyone has a cover story—a detailed explanation of who you are and who you are not. You formulate this "story" to satisfy what you understand to be your family's requirements. Because you base your cover on who you believe your family wants you to be, and not on who you actually *are*, your cover story isn't strictly accurate. In your cover story you admit to having certain qualities while you deny others. The qualities you acknowledge, your cover, are qualities you can use. The qualities you deny go under cover, and become unavailable to you.

This story generally works quite well within the context of your family, and as long as the changes you want to make require you to use only your cover traits, you can make them easily. But when what you want to do requires you to expose traits you've hidden under cover, you can get stuck.

EXPLAINING LIFE

You adopted your cover in early childhood as a way of explaining to *yourself* what was going on in your family. It answered your most important questions: "Why does Mommy act that way?" "Why am I treated this way?" "What will happen next?" As children we all need answers to such questions. Understanding what's going on around us is a basic human urge. Until our curiosity about our immediate surroundings is satisfied, we can't move on to tackle life's other puzzles.

Creating a cover answered your questions by defining you. "You're treated this way," your cover said, "because you're *smart, dumb, short, tall, weak, strong,*" and so on. The accuracy of the explanation was much less important than the fact that it explained things.

By explaining your immediate surroundings, even if you didn't like the explanation, even if it was the *wrong* explanation, your cover dispelled the mystery and confusion of daily life and freed you to turn your time and attention to other childhood challenges, like walking, talking, holding a spoon, reading, and growing up.

YOUR COVER STORY

Discovery is the primary task of childhood, and understanding their surroundings is children's full-time job. Figuring out how the world works is the natural occupation of children; finding fingers and toes, learning to walk and talk, coordinating eye and hand movements—all these activities require their undivided attention. When parents are stable, loving, and consistent, children can joyfully and single-mindedly pursue these activities. These children grow up believing that the world is a safe and abundant place that welcomes them just as they are. They needn't exaggerate what they *can* do or hide what they *can't* do. They believe that who they are is enough.

Children whose parents aren't stable, loving, or consistent have a very different experience. When parents are unpredictable, sick, unhappy, angry, preoccupied, neglectful, absent, or—

worse—abusive, children learn that the world is a dangerous place in which it isn't enough to be who they are. These children must figure out the correct, expected, or safe thing to be, and become it.

All children are sensitive to the needs of their parents. With amazing flexibility, they quickly figure out what pleases or displeases their parents and learn to do whatever is necessary. They will act smart, dumb, sick, well, responsible, or incompetent as required.

Beyond growing up, children have only one goal: to be the child their parents want them to be. Your cover is designed to protect you by convincing your parents that you are the child they want, or by helping you fit into your particular family structure. Unfortunately, most children believe that their lives depend on creating the perfect cover and hiding what they believe is undesirable about themselves safely under cover.

Sadly, parents sometimes prefer inadequate children, enjoying the feeling of personal power they get from the dependence of their children. Feeling inadequate themselves, such parents can experience the emerging strength of their children as a threat. Parents who need their children to be sick, dumb, sloppy, or incompetent find ways to make this known. Messages about who the child had better be or had better not be are clearly, if nonverbally, communicated, and children are in very little doubt as to what is expected of them.

WHO ARE YOU?

However you experienced the world as a child—whoever you were told you were, or decided you had to be—became your cover, which you retain to this day. If you were born to parents who didn't want to have children, you might see yourself as an intruder. If your parents had tried and tried to have children and finally had you, you might feel very special. There are as many possible covers as there are situations to create them. Your cover can be *inadequate, lucky,* or *fragile;* a *winner* or a *loser;* the *one who is saved* or the *one who is abandoned.*

Once you decide on your cover, it becomes the way you present yourself to the world. Without saying a word, you announce: I'm *pretty, ugly, interesting,* or *dull. Pay attention to me, ignore me, take care of me,* or *watch out for me.* I'm a *bully,* a *victim;* I'm the *audience,* or the *star.*

Your cover is so convincing that you act as if it's true even when it isn't. If your cover is *I try, but I don't succeed,* although you truly have the ability to succeed, you rarely do. Created while you were quite young, your cover is the hallmark of your adult personality.

Although Lance didn't realize it, the cover he created as a very little boy controlled many of the choices he made as a man. Lance was only five when his father left the family. After the divorce, his mother withdrew into herself, living increasingly in the past. Lance became his mother's "little man," listening to her complain about how badly his father had treated her.

Lance needed someone to take care of him, but his father was gone, and his mother needed *him* to take care of *her.* Lance knew that if he was needy or demanding he'd be like his "terrible father," who had hurt his mother and been sent away. Lance had no choice. He had to find a way not to feel what he felt, or need what he needed. He had to hide who he was and become the "little man" his mother wanted him to be. He needed a cover.

"The back bench, not the first string" is how Lance describes himself today. Women confide in him, telling him how badly they're treated by other men. He's always a best friend, never a lover. Lance chooses women who use him as a sounding board. He wants to have his needs met, but his cover—that he's the *support team*—"magically" draws him to women who, like his mother, are unable to give to him. Lance has the ability to have his needs met, but he doesn't use it. His fear—that if he puts his needs first, he will be rejected—keeps his cover firmly in place.

If your parents, like Lance's, were clearly inadequate to the task of raising a child, or if your childhood contained neglect, abandonment, trauma, or abuse, you can easily understand why you had to adopt a cover. But there are also many situations in which children misunderstand their parents' intentions and create covers where none were necessary.

CIRCUMSTANTIAL COVERS

Misunderstandings, circumstances, accidents, and events that were no one's fault can also cause you to create a cover. Sally's childish misunderstanding of her parents' intentions demonstrates this unfortunate phenomenon. When she was four years old, Sally's parents, afraid that she was too thin, took her to a doctor to fatten her up. Sally decided that her parents didn't want a thin daughter, so she gave them what she thought they wanted. At 40 Sally is still struggling with her lifelong weight problem.

Circumstantial covers can be very confusing to the people who have them, because sometimes what they believe about themselves—their cover—isn't based on events that happened directly to them. "Why should I be so scared?" they ask. "My parents were always kind to me." Younger children sometimes adopt *good, quiet, passive,* or *scared* covers after watching the punishment of an older child who was the *bad, difficult,* or *rebellious* one. Older children sometimes adopt *expendable, left-out,* or *unimportant* covers when a sibling born too close behind them captures the attention they needed to feel *important, valuable,* or *special.* Patty's *expendable* cover didn't match her memory of her childhood or her current relationship with her parents.

Patty described her childhood as "delightfully normal." Her parents loved her and treated her as though she was special. Why, then, did she feel *expendable?* Why was she so afraid of

49

being left that she often did things she didn't want to do just to please others?

When Patty was six months old, her mother became pregnant. Her mother was very ill during this pregnancy and couldn't care for Patty the way she wanted to. Her sister, Felicia, was a sick baby who required most of her mother's limited time and energy. To little Patty, it seemed that her own needs were unimportant.

Patty has a vivid memory that poignantly captures her cover: she's three years old and is riding in the car with the whole family. Everyone is in the front seat—her father driving, her mother sitting in the passenger seat with Felicia on her lap, and Patty sitting on the floor in front of the passenger seat. It's raining very hard and Patty hears the water splashing up against the wheels. She thinks, "If the water comes and pulls me away, no one will miss me." By the time she was three years old Patty had already developed an *expendable* cover.

Circumstantial covers can be difficult to recognize and take seriously, but covers created in a no-fault situation are just as debilitating as those built on solid fact. Without meaning to, a parent who gets sick or leaves to fight in a war can saddle a child with an *abandonment* cover. Although the parent didn't want to leave them, the children who are left think of themselves as *leavable*. For actor Gene Wilder, it was his mother's heart attack when he was eight years old that dictated the path his life would take.

In a television interview, Mr. Wilder talked about his mother's illness. He recalled that the doctor had cautioned him that if he got angry it could kill his mother, and that making her laugh would be good for her. This was a powerful motivation for Wilder's creation of his *I save lives with laughter* and *I never get angry* covers.

People who have circumstantial covers are in a double bind. When their lives stop working or when they hurt, they sometimes can't take their pain seriously because they can't see where it originated. "I had a very good childhood," they often say. "My parents loved me." Suffering from anxiety or depression, they come into therapy for help. But when confronted by the idea of the cover that is clearly driving them, they back off. They are unwilling to hold a parent who obviously loved them responsible for their adoption of a negative cover.

COVERS ARE STUBBORN AND SEDUCTIVE

Your cover continues to affect you long after the reason you adopted it—your original family—has stopped operating as a primary factor in your life. Even when you've had experiences that should have disproven your cover, this idea of who you are continues to determine what you believe is possible for you to be and do in life. That's because once you've successfully crafted your cover story and accepted that this is *who you are* and *who you aren't*, you forget that your cover is an invention of your own making. You come into adulthood believing your own cover story.

For example, when people with *fat* or *unattractive* covers suddenly lose a great deal of weight, they often complain that they still feel *fat* and *unattractive*. This is their cover talking, stubbornly clinging to the definition that protected them as a child. If the cover that protected you as a child disagrees with what you want as an adult, you can find yourself acting in contradictory ways. For 25 years Nancy's life belied her *outsider* cover, but when the circumstances were right, her cover resurrected itself.

Nancy's birth was an accident. Her parents were obsessed with each other and didn't want children. They were alienated from their families, friends, and their religion. Isolated from everything and everyone, they clung to each other. In the tight little circle they'd drawn for themselves, there was no room for Nancy, and from the beginning she knew that she was the *outsider*.

When she was four Nancy was hospitalized for six months. Her parents visited every week, but being literally outside the family only served to confirm Nancy's cover.

In her 20s she joined a radical political organization. She met and married an activist minister and had a child. Finally, Nancy had the home, family, and community she'd always wanted.

In her 40s, bored with her life, Nancy left her husband for a "more exciting" man. After seven years he still refuses to commit to a permanent relationship. Her husband quickly remarried and Nancy is now estranged from her daughter. She's lost all contact with her old friends and family because they really belonged to her husband. Today, at age 52, what she feels most strongly is that she is once again an *outsider*.

It's easy to see how Nancy re-created the experience of her early life and perpetuated her *outsider* cover. It's easy to criticize her and say, "Oh well, she didn't have to get involved with that other man." What is not so easy to see is how compelling the familiar can be, and consequently how irresistibly each of us is drawn to confirm the cover of our childhood.

The comfort of the *known* is seductive. Just the desire to avoid the unexpected can keep us from making changes that would enhance our lives. You may think, "Baloney, that's not a good enough reason to keep doing something that's hurting you." But the impulse to act in a predictable way so everyone else will continue to act in a predictable way is a very good reason to avoid change. Remember that you originally created your cover to guarantee your acceptance within your family. It was to assure the love and protection of your family that you disowned parts of yourself.

The urge to stay covered can be overwhelming. You may despise the cover your childhood forced you to accept as the truth. But as long as you believe that this cover is keeping you loved and safe, you'll continue to act in ways that perpetuate it. We all need to feel safe, to maintain the balance of whatever family we're in. If the change you want to make requires you to renounce your cover, and renouncing your cover threatens your safety, all attempts to force yourself to change will fail. If you notice that you're perpetuating a cover story you would like to abandon, for now, try to accept that you're still receiving some benefit from acting as if it's the whole truth.

UNDER COVER

Just as it protects you, your cover also limits you. *Pretending to be something you're not means denying something you are.* If your parents were comfortable only with *helpless* children, as a child you had to hide your *ability*. If they liked *smart* kids, as a child you always had to know the right answer and hide your *ignorance*. Feelings, behaviors, or qualities that would make you a child your parents wouldn't want became dangerous liabilities and remain so today. Whatever you believed you *had to be* became your cover. Whatever you believed you'd *better not be* became your under cover. Your cover is what you show, hoping it will bring you love and safety. Your under cover is what you hide, fearing it will cost you love and safety. Even though you gladly present the one and carefully hide the other, *both are true of you.* The artful and completely personal combination of the two is your cover story, the invention you told first to your parents, then to yourself, and finally to the world.

If, when you were small, you decided that a particular quality was bad and you successfully hid it under cover, then and now exposure of that quality is a danger you avoid at all costs. It's impossible to amputate feelings, behaviors, or qualities from our personalities. They all continue to exist within us, but we have a very human mechanism that allows us to think otherwise. Human beings all come well equipped with the capacity for denial.

WE ARE ALL CLEOPATRA—
THE QUEEN OF DENIAL

Denial is a natural defense mechanism, but this self-protective technique has been widely criticized lately. Denial is to the 90s what neurosis was to the 50s. In the 50s people said, "Oh, don't be so neurotic." Today they say, "Oh, you're just in denial."

It's incontestable that people do use denial in ways that endanger themselves and others: some refuse to use condoms, denying that they can become pregnant or get AIDS; some drive drunk, denying that alcohol affects their ability to drive; some deny their lover's past transgressions, assuring themselves that they won't be repeated. These are classic examples of the ways people use denial against themselves.

But while it is sometimes misused, the capacity to deny is necessary to our survival. None of us could get out of bed, much less drive a car or get into an airplane, if we couldn't deny the fragility of the body we inhabit and the dangers that exist all around us. How else could so many walk the dangerous streets of New York or live in earthquake-prone Southern California? It is our capacity to deny the very real dangers that surround us which allows us to go nonchalantly about our daily lives— making a living, falling in love, having lunch—as though the danger weren't there.

Occasionally an act of God, like a flood, or a personal tragedy, like the death of a loved one, will strip away our protective veil of denial and force us to recognize just how fragile we really are. Then we suffer insomnia, nightmares, flashbacks, and anxiety attacks. At those times we can't think about daily life—we lose interest in making a living or falling in love—because we're too busy worrying about our safety. But most of us are soon able to reweave our protective veil of denial and once again go obliviously about the business of our daily lives.

Denial is a lifesaver. It starts saving your life when you're very young by helping you pretend that you're not the child you are—the one your parents don't seem to want. In your first attempts to pretend, you may have said, "No, Mommy, I'm not sad, scared, or mad." These were lies, which, as a child, you may not have delivered too credibly. Eventually, however, you convinced yourself that this act was true. This act, which fools even you, is denial.

Your ability to deny the qualities that endangered your relationship with your parents allows you to forget, to this day, that you possess these qualities. But those characteristics— competence, sloppiness, intelligence, or sentimentality— haven't gone away; they've just gone under cover. Sometimes, as I pointed out in the last chapter, it is precisely these qualities, the ones you believe you don't have, that you need to change.

Brent badly needed his capacity to feel his very genuine sadness and fear, but his *pillar of strength* cover convinced him that he didn't possess these emotions.

At 45 Brent lost his arm in an automobile accident. He was healing medically, but not emotionally. A year after the accident, Brent reluctantly came into therapy. He was suffering from depression but he couldn't understand why he was depressed. He was, he said, the kind of person who assessed a situation, saw what needed to be done, and did it. He wasn't, he insisted, "someone who got bogged down in feelings."

Despite his denial, Brent was "bogged down in feelings." His *pillar of strength* cover stopped him from acknowledging the natural and appropriate grief, rage, and fear he felt over the accident and the loss of his arm.

Brent had been his mother's favorite child, but whenever he cried, she sent him to the "crying corner" until he stopped. From the "crying corner," Brent could see the pain on his mother's face. Even as a small boy he recognized that his sadness hurt her. At four years old, he determined never to cry again and to the best of his knowledge he never did. He became a *pillar of strength* for his fragile mom.

As an adult Brent had, with his wife, friends, and colleagues, re-created the balance he'd learned with his mother.

He cared for them and protected them from his pain. His cover served him well; he was successful, admired, and loved. Now, however, it endangered him. His fear of exposing his *I hurt* under cover to his current loved ones stopped him from feeling. "Pillars that sag or crumble are useless," he said, betraying his dreaded under cover of *I hurt* or *I lean on you* or, God forbid, *I cry.*

As long as Brent believed that the continuing love of his current family depended on his maintaining his pillar of strength cover, he didn't dare expose his *hurt* under cover. His need to deny that he hurt forced him to deny all of his feelings. His inability to feel caused his depression.

In therapy Brent realized that the *pillar of strength* cover he believed in so firmly as an adult had actually been created by a scared and loving little boy who felt responsible for an overwhelmed mother. Courageously, since he couldn't predict the outcome of this risk, Brent began tentatively to express his grief over the loss of his arm and share with his wife his fear about the future. To his amazement, she wasn't overwhelmed by his feelings as his mother had been. She didn't turn away or ridicule him. Instead she reached out to help him in ways he'd long since stopped believing were possible.

For Brent, the loss of an arm turned out to be a blessing in disguise. His accident gave him an opportunity to "un-cover" a depth and richness of feeling within himself that he didn't know he had. His courageous exposure of his heretofore hidden under cover allowed him to experience an entirely new relationship with his wife. She gave him comfort and support that he'd always denied himself in order to keep his *vulnerability* safely under cover.

Brent had been certain that he didn't experience sadness or grief. He didn't realize that he could feel these emotions and act in these ways. Perhaps you, too, are trying to become someone you already are. Qualities that you want, but think you can't attain, may actually be hiding under cover—waiting like Lana Turner at Schwab's—to be discovered.

UN-COVERING

To do all the things you are capable of doing, you must be all the things you are. This means you must pull off your cover and reclaim your under cover. However, as long as you think of the one as good and the other as bad, your taboo against un-covering will be very strong. As you search for yourself, try to keep an open mind about what you discover. Qualities you once thought of as bad, contemptible, or dangerous may actually be the ones you need to make the change you want to make. It may help to remember that all qualities, when viewed in the proper perspective, can be described in a variety of ways. *Recklessness* is often called *bravery*, and *stinginess* can also be seen as the desirable trait of *thrift*.

As Barbra Streisand pointed out when she was inducted into the Women in Film Hall of Fame, the same quality can have a vastly different meaning if it's applied to a man or a woman. She said, "A man is commanding—a woman is demanding. A man is forceful—a woman is pushy. He shows leadership—she's controlling. He's committed—she's obsessed. He's persevering—she's relentless. He sticks to his guns—she's stubborn."

EXERCISE—*Who Am I Really?*

If you're beginning to wonder what about you might be cover and what might be under cover, this simple exercise may help. Write two sentences that describe you, both of which begin with the words I am and are followed by a list of adjectives. Complete the first sentence with adjectives you like or approve of: I am *good, kind, pretty, smart*. Complete the second sentence with adjectives you don't like or of which you disapprove: I am *bad, selfish, stupid, ugly*.

Take your time doing this. It's simple, and its simplicity can be deceiving. Be creative and let your mind wander. Try not to censor yourself. You're not looking for the *right* answer but for the one your mind gives you. Be silly, frivolous, and inventive. Use as many adjectives as you can think of. The more spontaneous you are, the more likely you'll be to actually describe your cover and your under cover.

Another wonderful source of information about your cover and under cover qualities can be found in the stories about yourself that you enjoy telling and the ones that embarrass you. The things we choose to tell about ourselves can spotlight a cover, while the things we'd prefer to ignore can spotlight an under cover. For example, Sam always talks about deals he's closed but never about the ones that got away. He believes it's his *successful* cover that brings him love and admiration and that exposure of his *I can fail* under cover would take it all away. His wife, Rebecca, on the other hand, jokes about her bad judgment but never mentions the things she does well. She believes that it is her *inadequacy* that makes her lovable and that if she admitted her *competence* she'd be abandoned.

LISTENING TO YOURSELF

You can find clues to the identity of your cover story by simply listening to the way you talk to and think about yourself. Perhaps you don't realize that you can always tap into a constant stream of inner dialogue. Maybe you've never stopped to listen to and identify the way you talk to and about yourself. If you haven't, give it a try. We're all subject to this ever-present running commentary, by ourselves, to ourselves, about ourselves. Listen for recurring themes, phrases, and watchwords. Listen especially for your favorite clichés about yourself.

58

Do you often think of yourself as *caught in the middle*, a *lucky SOB*, or *always left out*? Do you *go for the jugular* or are you a *pushover*? Do things *just seem to work out for you*, or is there *a conspiracy against you*? These ways of describing yourself, even in jest, are often who you think you are or must be—your cover.

Contrarily, characteristics that you loudly declare are not true of you, as well as qualities you hide or deny, can point to your under cover.

Is there a nickname you're still trying to "live down"? Are there behaviors you engage in that deeply embarrass you? Did you once hold attitudes that you now prefer to forget? What things you've said or done in the past can still make you cringe? Is there a pattern or a common thread that runs through your answers? If so, it may point out a quality you think you must never display—your under cover.

If you discover under cover qualities that repel you, take heart. Remember that every quality can be described in many ways—positively or negatively. And bear in mind that you're probably thinking about these qualities from the perspective of a small child whose parents disapproved of certain behaviors. You're probably using labels you long ago attached to these traits, with little regard to their actual value. Brent believed that his under cover ability to *cry* and *need* would make him unlovable, but he was thinking of these qualities as the child had learned them, not as the adult would use them.

DON'T TELL MOMMA

Your under cover can also be found in the secrets you still keep from your parents. What truths about you would, even today, disappoint, upset, annoy, embarrass, scare, infuriate, or depress them? Sandy and Georgia are hiding *I'm sexual* under covers. At 30, Sandy is self-sufficient and living on her own, but she refuses to move in with her boyfriend because her parents would disapprove. Thirty-five-year-old Georgia makes her living as a writer of nonfiction magazine articles. She's working on a romance novel, but keeps it a secret because she's sure that the sexy parts would shock her religious parents.

Neither age nor distance limits our reluctance to expose our under covers to our parents. Every Sunday when his mother calls, 40-year-old Max lies and says that he's made his bed and is going to church, confirming his *good* and *religious* son cover. And at 85, Dr. Benjamin Spock could still recall the "terrified and trembling anticipation" with which he awaited his mother's reaction to the publication of his book *Baby and Child Care,* in which he'd exposed his *ungrateful* son under cover by criticizing her child-rearing practices. Dr. Spock was 45 years old at the time.

"THE LADY DOTH PROTEST TOO MUCH"

An important way to identify an under cover is to notice which qualities in other people make you angry or uncomfortable. In the family pie you saw how the despised qualities of another family member can be qualities you deny by hiding them under cover. Not only family members, but almost anyone who annoys or upsets you, can be demonstrating your under cover quality.

When we recognize our own hated under cover qualities in others, these otherwise carefully hidden aspects of ourselves awaken and vie for our attention. "That's me, too!" they scream. "Recognize me! Acknowledge me!" But as long as admitting to these qualities would put us in too much danger, we can't afford to recognize them. We must instead find some way to separate ourselves from these qualities. One of the ways we persuade ourselves that these qualities don't belong to us is by criticizing them when we spot them in others.

Before Elizabeth remembered the terrible sexual abuse she suffered at the hands of her uncle, she was cynical about those who claimed spontaneous recall of such events. Contemptuously, she accused other abused women of "making it up to get attention."

You can acquire valuable information about your under cover qualities by looking at those people who really make you uncomfortable—the character in a movie or a novel who makes your skin crawl, the relative you just can't bear to be around, the co-worker you don't know very well but are sure you don't want to get to know. What groups or kinds of people can't you help making fun of or ridiculing? Who turns you off, even when you can't think of any good reason that they should? Not only family members but friends and even strangers can be very useful in helping you ferret out your under cover. Lucy sneered at her neighbor for the *laziness* she was trying desperately to deny in herself.

Lucy was working too hard but couldn't make herself slow down. She was driven by her *conscientious* cover, which she believed was responsible for her success and the admiration of her colleagues. In a therapy session she suddenly began to talk about her next-door neighbor. "He's such a couch potato," Lucy complained. "He can spend an entire afternoon just sitting there watching TV. I don't know how he does it."

With this declaration Lucy distanced herself from this "couch potato–like" behavior, in so doing assuring herself that she would never commit such a sin. Lucy's parents had continually acclaimed her as *hardworking*, and condemned her brother as *lazy*. Lucy had kept her own ability to be *lazy* a secret, even from herself. As long as she couldn't afford to admit to her own *laziness*, criticizing this quality in her neighbor protected her from having to recognize it in herself.

The more passionately you react—the more black and white an issue seems to you—the more likely it is that you are in the presence of an under cover quality. Accepting, even considering, that these things may be true of you can be painful and scary. After all, you've probably devoted your life to keeping this disturbing quality a secret, even from yourself. You may still believe that your image, self-esteem, acceptance, or even your life depends on keeping this trait a secret.

Under covers are concealed because their exposure will put us in some kind of danger. In the above examples, Elizabeth's cynicism helped to shield her from the *hurt* and *scared* little girl under cover memories of her own abuse; and Lucy's denial of her *lazy* under cover protected her self-image, which was solidly based on her *conscientious* cover. You always have a good reason for hiding certain qualities under cover and continuing to present cover qualities—even when the one doesn't work and the other is needed.

INVISIBLE INK REASON

When Donna came to see me she was frantic. Her alimony was about to run out and she had to get a job, but she couldn't even make herself work on her résumé. Always a tireless volunteer worker who was much in demand, Donna knew she could get and keep a job. Friends and family who were once encouraging were hounding her to begin her job search. "What's wrong with me?" she asked.

It was Donna's *dependent* cover that was stopping her from looking for work. She'd modeled herself on her mother, who was, she said, "very capable, but completely dependent on my father." Like her mother, Donna kept her *competence* firmly under cover.

Donna's cover was supported and validated by her family's—not to mention her community's—belief that a woman should work for her family, friends, and community, but not for money. In return for all this work, women could expect to be loved, cared for, and supported. Consequently, Donna believed that getting a job and exposing her competent under cover would announce to the world her failure as a woman and cost her whatever love she might hope to have in the future.

When Donna discovered her cover she called it her "invisible ink reason." "Oh, I get it," she said. "There are all these reasons why you should do something, and then there's this one *big* reason why you shouldn't do it. Only it's written in invisible ink, so you can't see it. It's written in invisible ink because when you do see it, it's probably going to hurt. So it isn't until you can stand the hurt that you can find a way to read the invisible ink reason."

Donna had many good reasons for getting a job and only one "invisible ink reason" for not getting one—her belief that getting a job and exposing her *competent* under cover would cost her love and care. That reason was more than enough to keep her unemployed.

Donna's reluctance to expose her under cover confirms the toughness of the task we all face in un-covering and validates the protective intention we all have when we place a quality under cover. You can't admit to something you can't see! And when you can see it, when you're able to read your invisible ink reason, it's probably going to hurt. So, until you can bear the hurt, you won't be able to read the reason. And until you can read the reason, you won't be able to make certain changes in your life.

RE-COVERING

In order to be whole, to be your complete self and to make the changes you want to make, you must question your cover and recognize and integrate your under cover. But this process usually contradicts everything your personal history has taught you about what is safe.

You originally designed your cover to meet what you understood to be your parents' requirements. But as a child you had very little information. You may have misunderstood what they wanted or responded to an accidental circumstance. Or you may have understood perfectly what was required of you and created the ideal cover—but what worked then may not be working now.

A quality you've kept under cover for a lifetime may be the very one you need for the change you want to make today. That means that, without realizing it, you may be trying to turn yourself into someone you already are. You may be pursuing something you already have. The person you've been trying to become, the quality you've been trying to cultivate, may already be "right in your own backyard," right "under" your own "covers." You're probably tired and discouraged, having spent your most precious resources and seemingly having nothing to show for it. For a moment, give yourself a break . . . take a rest.

Attempting to unmask a cover and reclaim an under cover quality you've long denied is never an easy task. It's very difficult to surrender a disguise you believe is responsible for bringing you all the love and security you have. Now and then you may glimpse one or another of the qualities you've denied. You may get a hint of your ability to be *conservative, outrageous, difficult,* or *responsible,* for instance. But if you're not ready to survive the danger you'll face when you act out these qualities, you won't be able to acknowledge or utilize them. If you have begun to recognize some of your under cover qualities, perhaps the *laziness, sloppiness, self-confidence,* or *intelligence* you've kept hidden even from yourself, don't try to display them. For the time being just observe them from a safe distance and continue to keep the secret.

The idea that danger accompanies change is very real, and before you can risk making the dangerous changes, you need to know and prepare for the possible forms your personal danger can take.

Change Is
Dangerous

———

Before reading any further, take a minute to consider the idea that there is a danger attached to the change you want to make. When you think about making this change do you feel anxious? Is there a queasiness in the pit of your stomach or tension in your jaw or shoulder muscles? It isn't necessary to name the danger to recognize its existence. Even if you can't identify a specific danger or isolate the source of your anxiety, even if you think it's silly to suspect an unrecognized danger, consider the possibility that making this change scares you.

DIFFICULTY DOESN'T
GUARANTEE GROWTH

You may not accept the idea that some nameless threat can keep you from doing something you want to do. And the suggestion that it is fear of this danger that stops you may even make you angry. Culturally, we disapprove of avoiding danger; we call such behavior cowardice. We label fear a weakness. Capitalizing on our fear of fear, an underarm deodorant manufacturer chose the slogan "Never let 'em see you sweat" as the basis for their national ad campaign. In it, well-known celebrities proudly report that they pretend not to be afraid in situations where anyone would certainly have the right to be afraid.

We all grew up watching movies in which heroes like John Wayne and Gary Cooper bravely and often single-handedly courted and defied danger. We have a great deal of support for denying our fear but no models for accepting or dealing with it. Expressions like "hang tough" help us talk about courage, but our vocabulary for describing fear is insulting—"yellow," "sissy," or "chicken."

Our culture applauds the individual who struggles against impossible odds. Our country was founded on the premise that the weak will prevail against the strong. Even Dorothy, in *The Wizard of Oz*, proved that she, "the small and meek," could outwit Oz, "the great and powerful." We're all subject to a potent cultural mythology that encourages us to deny our fear and ignore any possible danger, a mythology that tells us

- ignoring danger defuses danger;
- recognizing danger causes danger to manifest itself;
- admitting fear incapacitates the individual; and
- difficulty guarantees growth.

Do you believe any of these myths? If you do, you may be trying to force yourself to make a change, just because it's a tough or frightening one. You may have focused all of your attention on the benefits you expect from the change and denied the possibility of danger. But

- ignoring your danger will not make it go away;
- recognizing your danger will not cause it to happen;
- admitting that you're afraid will not incapacitate you; and
- difficulty will not guarantee growth.

On the contrary, ignoring danger, denying fear, and trying to do something you can't do all guarantee failure. And failure, rather than advancing you, will set you back.

The ability to deny fear *will* keep you from feeling frightened, but as long as you pretend that danger doesn't exist, you won't be able to take your particular danger seriously. Recognizing your danger will help you prepare for it and allow you to appreciate your ability to protect yourself by avoiding it. The notion that protecting yourself by avoiding danger is something to be proud of may be a new concept for you. Raised in this "no guts, no glory" culture, you may be ashamed of your ability to shield yourself from danger. But your self-protective reflex to avoid danger is instinctive and natural. It is responsible for keeping the species alive. Our cultural tendency to condemn our natural instincts is one of the things that makes it so difficult for us to trust ourselves and search for who we really are. You will be more likely to make the change you want to make when you can trust that you're acting in your best interests and give up the impulse to second-guess or criticize what you do naturally.

CATASTROPHIC EXPECTATIONS

You may know exactly what you want to happen when you make a desired change, but no one can precisely predict the outcome of an action before it's taken. We can't forecast the result of the change we want to make, but we can imagine it, and when we think about the probable outcome of such a change, most of us envision our worst-case scenario, our "catastrophic expectations."

Catastrophic expectations stem from the belief that the worst thing that can happen, will happen, and—real or imagined catastrophic expectations have the power to keep us from changing.

ASKING THE WHAT IF? QUESTION

A good way to discover your catastrophic expectations is to ask yourself the "What if?" question: What will happen if I make this change? The answers you get may tell you exactly what is blocking your path to change.

Since you're asking this question about something you want to do, you may, at first, find yourself answering with positives. You may think, for example, that when you've changed you'll be happier, richer, prouder, safer, better liked, or that the change will bring you approval, employment, relief, satisfaction, security, love, or marriage.

After you've evaluated the bright side, look for the dark side, the disadvantages, the catastrophic expectations of the change you want to make: you may be busier, lonelier, more responsible, or more visible. You may have to perform, take risks, live up to your reputation, or say no. Others may judge you, expect more of you, be angry at you, or be surprised by you. They may be jealous, feel left out, or abandon you.

Marty was very surprised by the length of his list of catastrophic expectations. Previously, when he thought about the change he wanted to make, he had only come up with the ways it would enhance his life. Marty wanted to buy a house. Single and financially secure, he could easily afford to do so, but something stopped him. When I asked Marty what would happen if he bought his house, he first reiterated the positives: "I'd have a place of my own; I'd stop wasting the rent money; I'd have a garden; and I'd feel like an adult." Then, on second thought, he said, "But what if I lose my job? What if I decide to move out of state? What if I hate it after I buy it? What if I get married and my wife doesn't like it? What if I'm not cut out to own a house?"

These are Marty's catastrophic expectations. Far from trivial, they are very real concerns. If he buys his house, he may actually have to face some or all of these fears. As long as Marty can't bear to experience these possibilities, he won't be able to become a homeowner. Until he knows that no matter what happens, he can handle it, survive the experience, and go on with his life, Marty will continue to live in an apartment.

FAILURE

The most common catastrophic expectation, the one that's stopped us all at one time or another, is the fear of failing.

Successful people know that it is often necessary to fail before you can succeed. Rowland Barber, author and playwright, teaches his students that "you've got to write bad to write good." But for many people, just the possibility of failure is enough to keep them from trying.

Culturally we applaud success and disparage failure. Everyone knows that it's better to succeed than fail, right? Wrong! There are lessons that can be learned only from failure. Some people who start right out succeeding and consequently have no experience of failure are incapacitated later in life by their catastrophic expectation of what will happen if they do fail.

And as if the cultural pressure to succeed isn't enough, many people also have personal reasons for strenuously avoiding failure. For them, failure is linked to the loss of love. Many parents, in a mistaken effort to encourage their children, punish them for failing or reward them only when they succeed. This kind of parenting, however, teaches children that the price for failure is loss of love. None of us can afford to pay that price, so for those who believe that failure will cost them love, even thinking of a change that might end in failure is too big a risk.

Between the cultural and the personal pressure to succeed, many people are simply incapacitated by the prospect of failure—unable to do the things they really want to do for fear that they might fail.

It was Fran's fear that her marriage to Rick might fail that kept her from actually taking the plunge. When she came to see me, Fran had been dating Rick for two years. She was sure she wanted to marry him, but somehow couldn't make herself say yes. When I asked her why she didn't marry Rick, Fran had many reasons. But when she looked closely at her reasons, she admitted they "weren't substantial." Still, she was stuck.

When I asked Fran what would happen if she married Rick, she said, "I'd feel safer, my life would be more settled, and we wouldn't be paying two rents." Then, as though a light bulb went on in her head, she suddenly realized that she was afraid to fail. This would be Fran's third marriage and she wasn't sure she could bear to be a "three-time loser." Then, as quickly as it came, the awareness of how terrible it would be to be fail again began to fade and with a little laugh and a shrug Fran said, "Oh well, I'm sure it'll be okay."

But what if it's not okay? What if it *is* another failure? Before she can marry Rick, Fran must know that even if it is another failure, even if she experiences her worst catastrophic expectation, she will survive and not suffer too great a loss of self-esteem. Until then, her mouth can keep saying "It'll be okay," but she won't be able to make it say "I do."

SUCCESS

Success can also harbor catastrophic expectations because success can have unexpectedly dangerous or unpleasant side effects. As with failure, the price of success can also be loss of love. Expressions like "Don't get a swelled head," "You're too big for your britches," and "Who do you think you are?" make up the kinds of responses some people hear when they dare to aspire to, or actually achieve, success.

If the balance of your family—past or present—is upset by one of the members becoming *too* successful, success can bring scorn, criticism, jealousy, or ostracism. When success is your danger, you are doubly bound by the expected pain of failure or the expected cost of success.

Success as a catastrophic expectation can be much more difficult to identify. Brenda couldn't figure out what was stopping her from going after what she wanted until she realized that she had a catastrophic expectation of success.

Brenda was 41 years old. She'd raised her children and wanted to go back to work. She'd worked for many years before her marriage and was sure she could easily get a job. Competent, qualified, and encouraged by her husband, she still couldn't make herself take the first step toward finding a job.

It took Brenda a while to recognize that her catastrophic expectation was that although he encouraged her, she believed that her husband wouldn't like having a working wife and might divorce her. As long as she really believed that her success in getting a job might cost her her marriage, Brenda couldn't make herself look for the job she wanted.

When you first ask yourself the What if? question, you may get only a fleeting glimpse of your catastrophic expectations. Then, as a true product of your culture, you may find yourself thinking, "That's no big deal," or, "That shouldn't be stopping me," or even, "I should push through my fear." Friends may support your belief that your fear isn't a valid reason to hang back and not change. But trust yourself. For just a moment, allow yourself to consider that you really *are* afraid that something bad will happen when you make the change you've been avoiding. Accept that, however trivial it might seem to you and your friends at this moment, this catastrophic expectation is the reason you haven't been able to change—and that it's a valid reason.

71

PICK OF THE DANGERS

There are many kinds of dangers from which you may be shielding yourself, and the better you understand the nature of the danger you may have to face, the better prepared you will be to deal with it. In this section I will describe "future dangers" and "past dangers."

FUTURE DANGER

The easiest dangers to identify are the future dangers. These are the dangers that are present when you're trying to do something you've never done before. We all recognize that doing something for the first time—wearing high heels, cooking for your mother, traveling to a foreign country, or learning to operate a computer—can challenge us with unknown or future dangers.

THE GROWING EDGE. Imagine you're standing on a huge plot of land that ends at a cliff that seems to drop off into nothing; even when you're standing at the very tip you can't see what's below. The land represents your life up to the present moment. It contains all the things you've done—the changes you've already made and their consequences. Below are the things you haven't yet done—the changes you may want to make but haven't yet made, and their consequences.

The cliff that stands between you and what waits below is the "growing edge"—the place past which you've not yet ventured. Whenever you do something you haven't done before, you must leap off the growing edge into unknown future danger.

When you find yourself near the edge it's normal to be afraid because when you leap off the growing edge you can't know if you'll land on a pillow of clouds or a bed of nails. Until you know that you'll survive whatever you encounter, you won't be able to force yourself off the growing edge, no matter how unhappy you are with the status quo, or how much you believe you want to make the change.

Because approaching the growing edge is frightening in itself, many people spend their entire lives securely on the solid ground of the known. Sometimes they wonder what it would be like to jump, and daydream about the changes they would like to, but can't, make. Some people inch their way toward the edge only to scurry back to the security of familiar ground. It's clear from watching people endure boring, dead-end jobs and battering relationships that many feel forced to accept a known pain rather than risk an unknown danger they expect to be worse.

As long as you stay firmly on land, you're not in for any surprises. You know the results of any action you may take, because you've taken them all before. Life may be unpleasant or even painful, but it's a known quantity. It isn't going to surprise you. It won't expose you to an unfamiliar pain you didn't expect, don't know how to deal with, and may not be able to endure.

THE FRIGHTFUL UNKNOWN. When you try something for the first time, there is no way you can know what will happen. You may be expected to do things you don't know how to do; you may have to develop new skills; you may be surprised, caught off guard, or have your ignorance exposed. There can be real physical dangers involved when the change is something like learning to ride a bike, drive a car, play baseball, or ski. Changing careers, moving to another state, or going back to school can hold unknown and unpleasant surprises. First dates and first marriages are fraught with unknown dangers.

Opal was desperately unhappy, but her unhappiness wasn't enough to enable her to risk leaping off the growing edge. Opal

73

was unhappily married. She didn't love Roy and wanted to leave him, but she couldn't. Opal had moved from her parents' home to Roy's without ever having lived on her own. She was afraid that if she left Roy, no one else would ever love her and she'd be alone forever. Being alone, with all its terrifying catastrophic expectations, was a danger she didn't believe she could survive, so she stayed firmly, if unhappily, rooted to her plot of land with Roy.

Foolishness, embarrassment, helplessness, or feeling out of control are other powerful future dangers. If you have an *I'm in control* cover, if maintaining your *dignity* or being *on top of things* is important to you, the fear of unknown or future dangers can effectively stop you from doing things you want to do.

No matter how well you prepare, how hard you work, or how "good" you are, you can't guarantee the outcome of the risk you want to take. But people with *control* covers may find this idea very hard to accept. These people spend their time and energy trying to ensure their desired result. Writers write and rewrite, desperately trying to make their work perfect and unrejectable; lovers constantly assure themselves that this is Mr./Ms. Right and that all will be well. But no change comes with a guarantee; many times the worst really does happen— "perfect" works are rejected and "perfect" lovers disappoint us.

If you don't know that you will survive the "worst," it is too dangerous to take the risk. Until you can survive the danger, whatever it may be, *not risking* is the best, most self-protective choice you can make.

Are you standing at the growing edge, wanting to write a play, learn to drive, have a baby, or do some other thing you've never done before? Have you been obsessively trying to make sure that everything is perfect before you try, or have you been trying to peek over the edge to see what will happen when you jump?

If you suspect that the possibility of encountering a future danger is keeping you from changing, are you tempted to order yourself to "stop being so silly, and move forward"? Go ahead and give it a try. If you're successful—if you confront your future danger and make the change you want to make—*bravo!* But if you fail, be easy on yourself. It just means that this is too big a danger for you to tackle *at this time*. You'll make this change successfully when you can endure and survive the danger. In other words: When You Can You Will.

PAST DANGER

Future dangers threaten when you're going to do something for the first time. Past dangers threaten when the thing you want to do is something you've done before—something that had unpleasant consequences.

Perhaps you know the story of the cat who loved to sit on the stove and bask in the afternoon sun. One day when she curled up on the stove, she got burned. Uncharacteristically, someone was cooking in the afternoon. They never again cooked in the afternoon, but the cat never again risked the hot seat. We humans aren't so different from this cat. If badly enough burned, we may not be willing to risk the hot seat, no matter how temptingly the afternoon sun may beckon.

THE "DIVING BOARD." Imagine that you're standing on a very high diving board looking down at a tiny pool of water into which you know you must dive. The "diving board" is a safe, if restricted, place to stand; and the "dive" into the tiny pool is the change you want to, but can't, make. This is not a physical dive but an emotional one. It is the reliving of a painful past event you hoped you'd never have to experience again.

When the change you want to make requires you to relive a painful past experience, making the change means making that scary dive. Obviously, the prospect of making this dive is terrifying and a good reason to avoid making the change. In chapters 5 and 6, I'll explain how you cleverly manage not only to avoid diving but even to forget that such a dive is there to be made. This is because, as long as you can stay safely on the diving board, you needn't confront your past danger.

When you can't do something you always thought would come naturally, like making friends, finding love, or choosing a career, it may be that your reluctance to confront a past danger is stopping you.

Unpleasant past experiences become past dangers, but as I will demonstrate in chapter 5, experiences that are *too* painful are often hidden from ourselves. As a result, past dangers can be difficult to identify since they are based on unpleasant memories we frequently don't remember.

Whether we consciously remember the event or not, we base our expectation of what *will* happen primarily on what *has* happened. We compare what we're going to do to what we have already done. The more the event in the present resembles, duplicates, or suggests the event of the past, the more certain we are that the outcome will be the same. If, for example, your parents ridiculed your favorite toy or your special game, you may today have trouble choosing a career; if your early attempts to show affection were rebuffed, you may be afraid to offer your love today; if, on the other hand, you felt smothered by your parents' love, you may shy away from love offered by others.

If our past experience was pleasant, delightful, harmless, or fun, we look forward to the new experience that resembles it, expecting that it, too, will be pleasant and delightful. But if our past experience was unpleasant, difficult, hurtful, or damaging, we face the new experience that resembles it with distress.

THE FRIGHTFUL KNOWN. One of the most powerful past dangers blocking the path to change is that of "blowing your cover." The earliest lessons you learn in life teach you which truths about yourself will bring approval and which will bring rejection. The painful memory, conscious or not, of being

76

rejected because you were a *smart aleck* or a *crybaby* makes the prospect of being *too* smart or *too* sad a terrifying past danger. Any change that threatens to expose you as a *smart aleck* or a *crybaby* must then be avoided.

When you're surprised that you can't do the thing you want to do, when you expected it to be simple and are perplexed to find it difficult, when the thing you can't seem to do is something that others do easily, the past danger that is stopping you may be your fear of un-covering.

Raylyn came to see me because at 35 years old she wasn't married, and she wondered why. For most of her life, she hadn't thought much about marrying, assuming that it would happen in the natural course of events. Over the years, when her friends had been obsessed with dating and finding a man, Raylyn had teased and secretly judged them. Now, with most of her friends married or in serious relationships, she wondered what was wrong with her.

There was a very good reason why Raylyn had avoided the arena of love and commitment. Love and loving presented Raylyn with a frightening past danger, the risk of un-covering the fact that she was *imperfect*. Raylyn's father, whom she adored, was only happy when she was "his *perfect little girl*." When she was good, he loved and rewarded her; when she was bad, he punished and avoided her. But her father's ideas of good and bad weren't constant. Sometimes being "quiet as a church mouse" was the right thing to do, but other times it was the wrong thing to do. Little Raylyn could never relax. She could never risk just being herself. She created a *perfect* cover, but she knew that under cover she was *imperfect*, *bad*, and therefore *unlovable*.

Although she didn't consciously recognize it, Raylyn was sure that if she ever risked letting herself be loved, her imperfection would surely show, and it wouldn't be long before she'd lose that love. Before Raylyn could dive off her diving board into the dark and uncertain waters of love, she had to know that she could bear to be disappointed again. She had to know that if she should happen to pick someone who, like her father, had unreasonable expectations of a loved one and rejected her, she would survive the rejection.

Not only are we reluctant to expose aspects and characteristics of ourselves, but we are unwilling to show others our feelings. Expressing forbidden emotions is a potent past danger, one that forces many people to avoid making the changes they very much want to make in their lives.

THE DANGER OF FEELING

The spontaneous expression of emotion is for many a menacing past danger. The repression of emotion is well established in our society. Our pop songs reflect this very clearly. The Grammy Award–winning "Don't Worry, Be Happy" tells us to pretend to be happy; and Melissa Manchester's megahit "Don't Cry Out Loud," with the words "just keep it inside, learn how to hide your feelings," said it all.

We tell each other to "have a nice day," and when asked how we are, mechanically answer "I'm fine." This is such a reflex that if we get an unexpected answer we may not hear it. I once told a friend that it had been my birthday. He asked if I'd had a good time. When I said, "No, it was awful!" he automatically said, "That's good."

Do you dislike certain emotions? Are you embarrassed by, annoyed at, or judgmental of outbursts of anger or fear, your own or others? If so, then simply feeling may be your past danger.

FEELINGS, NOTHING MORE THAN FEELINGS. *You possess all the possible emotions.* Whether you recognize and express them or hide and deny them, you *can* feel joy, sadness, rage, contentment, fear, grief, despair, and delight—whatever human beings are capable of feeling.

You may have an *I never get angry* cover, but this only means that early in your life, when you expressed your anger, something happened that hurt, embarrassed, or frightened you. In self-defense you placed that anger under cover. You promised yourself you'd never expose it again and created a cover story that excluded it. The more painful the early experience, the more powerful your personal taboo against repeating it.

But feelings that you don't fully express don't go away, they go under cover. They're stored in a box on a back shelf of your psyche. Every time life calls for an emotion you don't have permission to feel, you add it to your collection. The unexpressed feelings remain a part of you, albeit a part you deny. Once you've successfully hidden these emotions you forget you ever felt them. You believe your cover, which says, "I just never cry," or "I don't remember the last time I got scared." Then, whether you realize it or not, you avoid situations that might elicit these dangerous feelings.

Our emotions are not our enemies, but rather our allies. Neither good nor bad, they are an essential part of being human. Just as sweating releases toxins from the body, so feelings release stress from the psyche. Exercise generates sweat. Living generates feelings: scary events trigger fear, heartbreaking events trigger sadness, and joyful events trigger happiness. We wouldn't ask a jogger not to sweat, or a person with a full bladder not to urinate, but we routinely ask ourselves and others not to feel.

THOSE FRIGHTFUL FEELINGS. If you have to avoid certain emotions, then you will have to avoid certain situations, too. If, for example, you can't bear to feel fear, you'll probably shy away from scary situations; if anger embarrasses you, confrontations may be out of the question. It isn't only the "negative" emotions people learn to deny; Maria's childhood taught her to disclaim joy.

When Maria came to see me she was physically exhausted. A very successful dress designer, she finally admitted that she was a workaholic. For years her friends had been telling her to take a vacation or at least lighten up, but she hadn't been able to slow down. When she was younger and less successful, she'd believed that what she called her "drive" was a blessing. It was, she was sure, responsible for her success.

At some point Maria had begun to grow suspicious of her ambition; perhaps, instead of her driving it, it was driving her. No amount of success seemed to satisfy her. She couldn't relax and enjoy her accomplishments. Rather, she immediately set higher goals and plowed herself back into her work. Now with her health on the line, she worried that she might not be able to stop.

In therapy I encouraged Maria to listen to her inner dialogue. To her astonishment, she "heard" herself curbing her joyful impulses. During a therapy session, as she talked about how "crazy" it was to stop herself from feeling joy, Maria suddenly remembered her mother saying that "pleasure was the work of the devil and would be punished by a vengeful God." It wasn't Maria's love of work that was driving her, it was identification with her mother, which made her resist feeling her own happiness.

If expressing an unacceptable emotion is your past danger, the events of the present that provoke this past danger don't have to duplicate the event of your past to trigger the forbidden feeling. The present event that was stimulating Angie's past danger bore no resemblance to the event in her past that had created it. Angie came to see me to solve a problem with writer's block. A successful screenwriter, she'd been asked to develop a project about a depressed teenager. Always prolific and self-disciplined, Angie suddenly found that she just couldn't make herself sit still, much less write.

In her therapy session Angie talked in a random way about her early life until she got to her mother's death when she was 14. Then she started to cry uncontrollably. Angie was astonished. "I didn't think this still hurt me," she said. "I never think about it anymore."

After her mother died, Angie was sent to live with her grandparents. They were kind, but unable to comfort a frightened and confused teenager. Angie found a way to bury her grief and sorrow. Consciously, she believed that she'd "dealt with it." Now this assignment, in which she had to probe the feelings of a depressed teenager, threatened to unearth all the terrible pain and suffering of her own past.

Fear of experiencing the hurtful feelings she'd had to deny as a child stopped Angie from doing her work. When she saw the connection, she began to use her therapy sessions to express the grief she'd long denied. As soon as she began to address this problem, her writer's block disappeared.

AM I LOSING MY MIND?

Past emotional dangers are especially frightening because you experience them in the present exactly as you experienced them in the past. When an event in the present triggers an emotion you buried in the past, you feel the emotion now exactly as you felt it then. Although the incident that hurt or scared you happened many years ago, you react as though it's *happening now*. Since nothing that is actually happening in the present can account for the reaction you're having, you may worry that you've gone crazy. Then you not only feel an emotion you despise or fear, but you may also think you're losing your mind.

When Elaine came to see me she was desperate. She couldn't figure out what was wrong with her. She loved her husband, Carl. Although she was aroused by him and wanted to make love to him, whenever he kissed her on the mouth, or put his arms around her in a certain way, she felt as though she was suffocating and involuntarily pushed him away.

Elaine was only four years old when an older boy from the neighborhood cornered her in the basement and smothered her little body with his. The combination of his weight and her fear made it hard for her to breathe.

By the time she was four years old, Elaine had adopted an *I'm fine* cover because she already understood that her parents didn't like "whining, crying little girls." Elaine couldn't risk "blowing this cover" and exposing herself as *hurt* or *scared*, so she never told anyone what happened to her. Instead she found a way to hide her feelings of terror and shame and to forget that the abuse had ever taken place.

Now, many years later, the pressure of Carl's body on hers threatened to bring back that childhood memory and her terrible feelings. Until she could bear to confront these feelings, Elaine couldn't risk the behaviors that might trigger them; but since there was nothing in her present life or in her memory of the past to explain this overreaction, Elaine worried that she was losing her mind.

The terror, shame, and rage that little Elaine felt were normal. If she'd been comforted by a loving adult and able to voice them, these emotions would have been released and allowed to fade away. But her fear of becoming the "whining little girl" her mom and dad didn't like forced her to bury her feelings and turned them into dangers she had to avoid.

When her husband embraced her, the feelings of a terrified little girl came flooding back. Simultaneously, the certainty that if she expressed these feelings she'd be punished as a "whining little girl" also flooded back. Elaine *became* that little girl and was overwhelmed by the power of her feelings. With no understanding of what was happening to her, Elaine reflexively backed away from any kind of sexual activity.

I assured both Elaine and Carl that Elaine wasn't losing her mind; that fear of reexperiencing something terrible was probably causing her unusual behavior; that this was something that occurred in the past, and although it would undoubtedly be unpleasant to reexperience, it would in no way damage Elaine; and that my office was a safe place for her to experience it.

Elaine was finally able to remember the incident that caused all of this pain and allow herself to rage and grieve—to let loose the feelings she'd so long denied. She was able, over time, to fully express the emotions she'd withheld. And then, with Carl's help and understanding, she was able to enjoy a satisfying and happy sex life.

Important changes trigger powerful emotions. If the change you want to make will expose you to too terrible an emotional past danger, you won't be able to make the change until you can stand to relive the emotion. As long as the change you want to make threatens to provoke a feeling you literally cannot bear to face, you'll continue to protect yourself by not changing.

EXERCISE—*Name That Feeling*

Recognizing the emotions you resist or shy away from can help you decide if an emotional past danger is blocking your path to change. Do any of the following ring a bell for you?

- Do loud or angry voices scare you?
- Does the thought of crying or yelling make you queasy?
- Are you uncomfortable or embarrassed when accused of being, or caught acting, sad or ecstatic?
- Do you deny feeling lonely or angry or scared?
- Do you say things like "Getting angry won't help"?
- Do you use loaded words like "chicken," or "wimp"?
- Are you concerned about appearing foolish or out of control?
- Can you remember the last time you cried?
- Does it still make you blush?
- Is it painful for you to see a friend or loved one acting sad or scared?

- Do you discourage others from expressing certain feelings?

- Do you say things like "Don't cry, it just makes things worse," or "Don't feel bad, everything will be okay"?

- Do you shut your children down with phrases like "Big boys don't cry," or "Go to your room until you feel better"?

Asking yourself these kinds of questions can help you discover which emotions you feel comfortable expressing and which ones you prefer to leave in the box.

The first step to taking your feelings seriously is to figure out what they are. This means simply noticing them as they occur: identify your feelings *as you have them*. When you detect a feeling, note it. Say to yourself, "Aha, I'm feeling scared or mad or anxious." Or, you might have to say, "I think this is sadness or anger or apprehension," or even, "I wonder what this feeling is?"

In our busy lives, most of us brush our feelings aside as quickly as we can. We pretend, to ourselves and to others, that we're not hurt, angry, scared, or embarrassed. We place great value on being cool and in control. If you're like most people, you've spent your life trying to deny at least some of your feelings, and you won't be able to turn all that energy around in a day or two. You may find that you've forgotten to do the exercise—or you may remember the exercise, but be unable to identify the feelings. Go easy on yourself. When it's safe for you to experience the feelings you've had to deny, you will.

If you do begin to feel an emotion you previously denied, don't *do* anything differently at first. Don't try to alter the way you act or behave, just notice what you're feeling and when you're feeling it. If, although you are definitely *not trying* to express these feelings, they begin spontaneously to creep into your emotional repertoire, don't panic, try to enjoy them.

If you suspect that the possibility of encountering a past danger—the blowing of your cover story or the spontaneous expression of a forbidden feeling—is keeping you from doing what you want to do, you may want to try to do it anyway. Go ahead. But if, having given it your best effort, you still can't make yourself do it, don't be hard on yourself. You're probably underestimating the pain you'll have to face when you are finally able to dive off the diving board and make this change.

Your
Unconscious—
A Friend in Need

Until now I have defined the obstacles to change: the power of your family, your need to create a cover story, and the dangers you will face when you change. In your struggle to change, however, you also have an advocate, a silent partner, that actively protects you from danger. This ally is your unconscious mind.

Actually you have two minds—a conscious and an unconscious. Both your conscious and your unconscious minds provide you with ideas, skills, facts, memories, and solutions to problems, but they operate very differently in your life.

You are no doubt already familiar with your conscious mind, which communicates with you via *thought or awareness*. When you're thinking or making plans, you're using your conscious mind. It is the conscious mind that most of us think of as "me."

You may not be familiar with your unconscious mind, however, or know how it operates in your life. Your unconscious mind uses your behavior to communicate with you. When you say or do something you don't understand, can't explain, or couldn't have predicted, you're using your unconscious mind. When using their unconscious minds, many say "I wasn't myself," or "That wasn't me talking," or even "I didn't recognize myself." Your unconscious mind can bypass your conscious mind. Since your conscious mind is the seat of your awareness and the way you know yourself, when your unconscious mind participates in your life, you may feel that your life is somehow out of your own control.

Even if you're familiar with your unconscious mind, far from considering it an ally, you may think of it as anything from an annoying kibitzer to a dangerous intruder. It can be difficult for people raised in our goal-oriented society to appreciate that part of themselves that stops them from reaching their goals. The intention of this chapter is to demonstrate that the very behavior for which your unconscious mind is most often condemned—blocking the path to change—is actually the very behavior for which it should be applauded.

YOUR "GOOD" MIND
VS. YOUR "BAD" MIND

Because we recognize and can observe the workings of the conscious mind, it is valued in our culture. We take the information coming from the conscious mind, which is also called the analytical, rational, sensible, logical mind, or the left brain, very seriously. And since we can't observe the workings of the unconscious mind (and indeed many deny its existence), it is undervalued. The information that comes from the unconscious, which is also called the irrational, illogical, emotional, intuitive, instinctual mind, or the right brain, is often spurned, discounted, or completely disregarded.

Although they operate very differently in your life, both of your minds help you make changes in your life. Changes that don't endanger you, that won't "blow your cover" or expose you to a future or past danger, are the responsibility of your conscious mind. Your left brain is clever and resourceful and helps you accomplish many of the things you want to do. Your conscious mind contains all of your analytical skills and uses them to solve your problems. But your conscious mind doesn't know everything about you. It is unaware of the traits and memories that, in self-defense, you have had to deny.

Whenever you experienced an event or a feeling that was too painful for you to tolerate or whenever you recognized something about yourself that was too dangerous to reveal, you hid it. You not only hid it from others, *you hid it from yourself,* from your conscious mind. Your unconscious mind is the keeper of these dangerous secrets and will hold them under wraps until you can bear to "know" them.

Recognizing and protecting you from danger is the job of your unconscious mind. It hides the dark mysteries of your life from everyone, including your conscious mind. Your conscious mind may be encouraging you to leap off the growing edge into future danger or dive off the diving board into past danger, but it can only do this because your conscious mind doesn't see the danger. When your conscious mind says, "It's no big deal, go ahead and jump," it's your unconscious that sees the danger and stops you.

It obstructs any changes your conscious mind tries to force you to make before you're ready. But when you're ready to change, when you can tolerate the information you've previously hidden away, your unconscious will help you make these changes even if you don't know you're ready to make them.

WHO WAS THAT?

Changes you are ready to make, but don't realize you *can* make, are the responsibility of your unconscious, as it can alter your behavior without the consent or even the awareness of your conscious mind. Your unconscious can cause you to say things you didn't mean to say and do things you didn't mean to do. Have you ever heard yourself saying something you immediately wanted to stuff back in your mouth? Many clients have confided to me in the privacy of a therapy session that they were astonished and appalled to "hear" their mouths saying "Yes, I'll marry you," while their minds were saying "No!"—or vice versa.

Your unconscious can alter what you think and what you remember, as well as what you say and do. Many years ago I scheduled a job interview for 3:00 on Monday. When Monday came, however, I somehow remembered that the interview was at 4:00. Halfway there, I realized my mistake. I arrived at 4:00. Because I have a *responsible* cover, confusing the appointment time was so unusual that I knew my unconscious was giving me a message. "Don't take this job," it seemed to be saying. I didn't consciously know why, but I trusted my unconscious and believed that there was indeed a good reason to avoid taking this job. So I apologized for my tardiness, but I didn't make another appointment.

I sometimes tell this story to clients who are skeptical or afraid of their unconscious minds. I encourage them to be on the lookout for the surprising interventions their unconscious may devise, such as slips of the tongue, "slips of the mind," and behaviors that are unexpected or out of character. I encourage them to expect their unconscious to aid them in unforeseen ways. When I told Wendy this story, she said that such a thing couldn't possibly happen to her, because she was "too well organized."

Wendy had complete confidence in her conscious mind and her *trust me, I'm in control* cover. She was astonished when, for three weeks running, she got our appointments wrong. She came on the wrong day, at the wrong time, or forgot it completely. Wendy's unusual behavior scared her. She thought she was losing control.

When she recognized the specificity and elegance of the choice made by her unconscious, however, she was amazed. Far from being out of control, Wendy's unconscious was controlling the situation perfectly. It was duplicating exactly the example I'd given her about getting my appointment time wrong; the one she consciously believed "couldn't happen to her." Wendy resisted accepting that her unconscious could orchestrate her forgotten appointments, but the minute that she did, she stopped getting them wrong.

Understanding that her unconscious could act on her behalf changed Wendy's self-image. She'd always thought of herself as someone who had to struggle, to keep a tight grip on the reins of her life. She believed she needed to stay in control. Wendy had come into therapy to "lighten up," to find a way to relax and enjoy her life. Before she could risk making this change Wendy had to know that she could trust herself. As long as she believed she was limited to her conscious talents, she felt compelled to stay vigilant. By demonstrating its power to act in her life, Wendy's unconscious was encouraging her to "lighten up."

Do you think of yourself as a no-nonsense, logical person? Do you pride yourself on your ability to reason, analyze, or figure things out? Do you say things like "I only believe in what I can see," or "There has to be a logical explanation"? Have you ignored or even ridiculed information which came to you or others from alternative sources, impulses, dreams, feelings, hunches, or intuitions? If so, you're probably primarily, or even exclusively, identified with your conscious mind.

The conscious mind, with its logical and analytical skills, is a very valuable tool, but it's not the only one you have. If it's the only one you recognize, you're shortchanging yourself. If, like Wendy, you believe it's your only resource, then you may be cheating yourself out of a very important asset.

Your unconscious mind *can* contain disturbing information, such as despised under cover qualities, dangerous emotions, and frightening memories. As long as you can't bear to acknowledge this painful information, your unconscious will keep you from recognizing it. If the change you want to make—applying to graduate school, filing for divorce, or getting a job—threatens to expose some of this information before you can tolerate it or put it to good use, your unconscious *will* stop you from making that change.

Until you understand that your unconscious is protecting you, you may think of it as an enemy, a saboteur, or guerrilla fighter who is undermining you from within. But believing that your unconscious is the enemy only condemns you to fight a war you cannot win—a war against yourself.

CIVIL WAR

When you want to change but can't, and you don't realize that there's a good reason for this, you may feel frustrated and want to blame someone. If you don't realize that it's your ally, you may blame your unconscious for the trouble you're having. After all, you know that your conscious mind isn't stopping you. Your conscious mind can see only the advantages of the change and clearly wants you to make it. The culprit must therefore be that sneaky, out-of-sight part of yourself, your dreaded unconscious.

Shifting the blame off your conscious shoulders can make you feel better. It's not *your* fault you're stuck—at least not the *you* you know. But as long as you think of a part of yourself as the enemy, you're fighting a "civil war." You're at war with yourself. If you're being attacked—stopped from doing what you want to do—you must counterattack. But whom do you counterattack? The enemy, the one who's stopping you, of course. But the one who's stopping you is *you*.

These attacks often take the form of brutal self-criticism: "Shape up," you demand of yourself. "Stop being so stupid, lazy, silly, and self-destructive!" Unfortunately, criticism rarely has the desired effect. Such attacks, which were intended to motivate you, just leave you feeling beaten up. They waste your time and lower your self-esteem. Then, seeing that you've once again failed to do what you want to do and feeling that you've let yourself down, you may again accuse yourself of being the enemy and launch a fresh attack. Anything can become the basis for a civil war. Aspects of life that many would view as insignificant can be viewed by others as critical. By the time Pam came to see me she had turned a tug-of-war over being on time into Armageddon.

Pam came to see me complaining of chronic lateness. No matter what she did, she couldn't get anywhere on time. Whenever she had an appointment, she spent the day worrying that she'd be late and ordering herself not to be. Somehow, despite her best efforts, she'd get distracted; and before she knew it, she was late again. As she drove to her appointments she scolded herself. When she arrived, she was too upset to do business or enjoy lunch. On the way home she hammered at herself again, but none of this punishment kept her from being late the next time.

By the time she came to see me, much of Pam's life was being spent in a "take no prisoners" civil war with herself over her lateness. She spent hours worrying about the times she'd been late, dreading the times she'd be late again, desperate to change this behavior, and merciless in her self-criticism.

Pam's conscious mind, seeing only the pain caused by being late, scolded, criticized, and berated her. But as Pam discovered, even the most unforgiving civil war won't get you what you want. Self-reproach won't convince your unconscious to let you change before you're really ready.

Pam's unconscious mind knew that she wasn't yet ready to unbalance her families, original or current. That balance depended on her maintaining an *incompetent* cover. Her husband, Barry, a successful stockbroker, was proud of his ability to take care of his "delightful if ditzy" wife, and her parents took pleasure in now and then "slipping her money, just in case."

Unconsciously, Pam knew that her parents and her husband needed to see her as *incompetent* so they could continue to see themselves as *caring* and *generous*.

Pam was actually a very bright, talented, and creative woman with a long list of impressive accomplishments. But in describing herself, she downplayed her achievements and spotlighted her failures, primarily her failure to be on time. Although clearly untrue, Pam believed in the *incompetent* cover she presented.

However much she consciously wanted to change, for the present, the pain of feeling incompetent was preferable to that of upsetting her loved ones by demonstrating that she really didn't need them to take care of her.

When your unconscious stops you from making a change you're consciously certain you want to make, it always has a very good reason, often a reason relating to maintaining the balance of one or more of your important relationships. Simply recognizing this to be true can make it possible for you to disengage from the civil war you may be waging, a battle that will gain you nothing but increased discomfort.

A war against yourself is a war you can't win. It can only sap your energy, confirm your worst beliefs about yourself, and cheat you out of whatever opportunity you have to enjoy yourself.

CEASE FIRE

If you're engaged in a civil war with yourself it's because you incorrectly perceive your conscious and your unconscious minds as enemies. Your conscious mind is the commander of the attacking army, but it isn't trying to undermine you, it's trying to motivate you. Your unconscious mind is the commander of the defending army, but it isn't trying to undermine you, it's trying to protect you.

Consider disengaging, even temporarily, from this conflict by intercepting the critical missiles you throw at your self-esteem. Reread the Listening to Yourself section in chapter 3 to recognize when and how you do it. Then, try to catch yourself in the act of self-criticism and, if you can, interrupt it. This is not as easy as it sounds. I suggested to Miriam that she try it, but when she came for her next session, Miriam was puzzled. "I don't know why you asked me to do that exercise," she said. "I never call myself bad names. I paid attention and found that I only give myself encouraging and loving messages." Miriam was profoundly surprised when I pointed out, later in the session, that she'd just hit herself in the head and called herself a "dummy."

Perhaps like most of us you've been fighting civil wars over one issue or another all of your life, blaming yourself for whatever went wrong in your life or for whatever you couldn't do or couldn't do well enough. If so, scolding yourself may be such a well-established reflex that, like Miriam, you won't even be able to catch yourself in the act, much less interrupt it.

If you find you can't do this now, forgive yourself. For some of us the civil war reflex is too well entrenched, too much a part of who we are, to change overnight. And your *inability* to perform this exercise will provide you with a wonderful opportunity. It gives you a chance to resist using your difficulty with this exercise as ammunition for your next battle.

MCDONALD'S WAS RIGHT, YOU DO DESERVE A BREAK

The world can be a harsh taskmaster, insisting on performance and judging failure harshly. But if, after a grueling day of dealing with an uncompromising world, you come home to another adversary—yourself—there's no place you can rest. When you're at war with yourself the enemy is always there, armed and dangerous.

You need and deserve a safe place to retreat, recoup, rejuvenate, and prepare to meet the world's demands. But when you're engaged in a civil war, instead of the comfort, rest, soothing, and encouragement you need, you receive scorn and derision. This can turn your life into an endless series of tests and challenges. Competing, defending, explaining, and worrying are all you do. Instead of helping you reach your goal, the civil war disables you. The constant fighting drains you of precious energy. It leaves you less able to pursue the change you want to make or to enjoy the pleasure you might be having in the meanwhile.

If you realize that you've been fighting a futile civil war, and you've been able to interrupt hostilities, reward yourself. Breaking—or even denting—the lifelong habit of self-criticism isn't easy. Take yourself to the movies, stop reading this book for now and pick up your favorite novel, or just go for a walk. Give yourself a reward for a change.

YOUR UNCONSCIOUS BAG OF TRICKS

Your unconscious is ingenious and clever. It has the most creative and surprising techniques to use on your behalf. Do you know *your* unconscious's favorite way of communicating with you?

- Do you get sleepy when you don't want to do something?
- Are you always late to places you don't really want to go?
- Do you get hunches or strong feelings about things?

Following are some of the most common methods used by the unconscious mind to inform us of its intent, but this list is by no means exhaustive. Everyone's unconscious is unique and each has its own person-specific ways of making its point. Some of these methods may fit you, and some may not.

My own unconscious, for example, frequently speaks to me through music. Consequently, I pay close attention to the songs I find myself humming and the tunes I just can't get out of my head. When I was interning to become a psychotherapist, "I," my conscious mind, believed that I should be able to help anyone who came to see me. I was assigned to work with a very troubled young woman. I felt too inexperienced to help her, but my conscious mind kept insisting I should be able to do it. I was very torn and couldn't decide what to do until I "heard" myself humming the song "Go Away, Little Girl." I promptly referred her to a more experienced therapist, acting on the message from my unconscious.

As you read on, keep in mind that your arrangement with your unconscious may be different from any I mention here. If you're curious and open to self-exploration, you may discover a whole world of information about yourself that you never suspected.

MIXED MESSAGES

When the demands of your conscious mind are in direct opposition to those of your unconscious mind, you are literally of two minds. And these two minds may have very different agendas. No wonder you're confused! As you can see from the "civil war" section, your two minds can actually give you mixed messages. You can *think* you want to do one thing and find yourself *doing* another. When your actions run counter to your beliefs, you may be tempted to discount your actions. It's a cliché, but *actions can speak louder than words*.

The "Freudian slip" is a good example of the ability of your two minds to give you mixed messages. When you make a

Freudian slip, you *intend* to say one thing but actually *say* another. Your unconscious mind uses your own words to tell you something about yourself. This can be something you don't "know" about yourself, like the exposure of an under cover quality; it can be something you'd rather not know, such as the recalling of a traumatic event; or something you know but would rather not admit, as when a secret critic of Sigmund Freud introduced him as "Dr. Fraud."

The following are two examples of Freudian slips made by people who were unaware that they'd made them. What do you think they indicate about the people who made them?

Alex congratulated Charles, who had entered the seminary, on having entered the "cemetery."

Jack continued to sing "hurt my healing heart," when the lyric read "heal my hurting heart."

If you have the courage to honor rather than discount your actions that *contradict* your beliefs, you may find that your unconscious has buried an important message in the action. Eve was plagued by an embarrassing and stubborn Freudian slip, which she tried to but couldn't ignore. At first she didn't even realize that she called her mother her sister and vice versa. When I pointed it out, Eve was embarrassed. She didn't understand why she did it and she wanted to stop. But even when she was fully aware of the slip, she couldn't make her mouth stop saying it.

Eve's mother was an alcoholic who treated her children as pals. Eve's real caretaker was her older sister, Arlene. Arlene did as good a job as she could, but she was only three years older than Eve, and there were many things she couldn't do. This meant that many of Eve's needs were ignored or neglected. Early in her life, Eve adopted an *I don't have needs* cover to protect herself from the pain of being neglected, which she felt but didn't dare to express.

Now Eve wants a raise at her job. She knows she deserves it, but her boss won't volunteer it. Eve must ask for her raise, but to do this she'll have to renounce her *I don't have needs* cover, and accept her *needy* under cover. When she thinks about asking her boss for a raise, her cover kicks in and she protects him exactly the same way she protected her mother. "He has so much on his mind," she says. "I don't want to bother him."

Before Eve can ask her boss for a raise, she has to know that her needs are as important as his, but acknowledging this would put Eve in past danger. Eve will be in danger of recognizing how her mother failed her and how her childhood needs were neglected.

When Eve recognizes this truth, she may get back all the feelings that she buried when she first felt the pain of needing, but not having, a mother. If she does recover these feelings, she will feel them in the present exactly as she felt them in the past. She'll *be* a hungry six-month-old who isn't getting fed, or a frightened two-year-old who has to cry herself to sleep. Until she can bear this pain, her unconscious keeps her secret by letting her believe in the *I don't have needs* cover that protected her then and is protecting her now.

Like Eve, you may discount the mixed messages you receive from yourself. You, too, may try to ignore actions you don't understand or that embarrass you. But such actions can be useful sources of information, even when they seem to contradict one another. As the poet Walt Whitman wrote in his epic poem "Song of Myself," "Do I contradict myself? Very well then I contradict myself. (I am large, I contain multitudes.)"

FORGETTING TO REMEMBER

Another of the unconscious mind's favorite tricks is helping us forget to remember. Like Freudian slips, this is a common occurrence, something we've all experienced, but which most of us discount. Have you ever

- forgotten the name of someone you know quite well, just as you'd begun to introduce them;

- torn apart the drawer or purse where you *know* you put your keys, and can't understand why they aren't there; or

- tried to dial a telephone number you've dialed a hundred times, but suddenly can't recall?

Yes, sometimes this just means that you've got too much on your mind, or that you're distracted. As Sigmund Freud is supposed to have said, "Sometimes a cigar is just a cigar," and not a phallic symbol. But forgetting to remember can be a message from your unconscious that means something quite different—as when a client of mine forgot my name while introducing me to her mother, who disapproved of therapy and didn't know the role I played in her daughter's life.

Carla came into therapy to "make peace" with her parents. She'd gone to lunch with a friend and was discussing her mother and father, when her friend made a surprising observation about Carla's relationship with her parents. Carla promised herself that, at our next session, she would tell me what her friend had said. When the time came, however, while she could recite the whole conversation, Carla couldn't recall the "important part."

Carla was very annoyed by this demonstration of her ability to forget to remember; her conscious mind wanted to know the thing she'd forgotten. Her annoyance turned to admiration, however, when she realized the remarkable talent her unconscious had displayed. It had demonstrated its power to conceal information that her conscious mind had already seen. It was one thing for Carla to hear this from a friend; quite another to explore it with her therapist.

To Carla, who'd always been skeptical about the existence and power of her unconscious, the experience of having it act spontaneously on her behalf was a wonderful surprise.

THE WANDERING MIND

Your conscious mind, believing that your safety depends on its knowing whatever there is to know, can be unrelenting in its search for information. Pressed by their conscious minds, many people feel that they must stay present, attentive, or alert; and they are annoyed with themselves, or even frightened, when they space out, zone out, or lose touch.

But one of the most powerful tools used by our unconscious is its ability to shield information from the prying eyes of the conscious. After a month in therapy, Joel asked if he could sit in another place in the room because he was distracted by the big tree outside the window. "Sometimes I just can't stop looking at it," he said, "and I want to pay attention to what you're saying." I explained to Joel that his unconscious was carefully monitoring everything I said, letting him hear some things and distracting him from others. It would divert his attention, for example, when he was overwhelmed or overloaded, when I was saying something that his conscious mind didn't need to know, or when his unconscious mind decided that *it* wanted his attention. At these times it would shift his attention, suddenly making him very interested in the tree. I assured Joel that sitting in a different seat wouldn't change anything, because if his unconscious wanted to distract him, it could just as easily cause him to be fascinated by his fingernails.

As a therapist I am always on the lookout for those moments when someone shifts his or her attention from listening to me to listening to themselves. I told Joel, as I tell everyone who comes to see me, to value these moments of inward focus as opportunities to "hear" from their own unconscious, and the information their unconscious mind provides is more valuable than any information I can offer. At these moments, if I ask where they've gone, some people react like school children caught not "paying attention" to the teacher. They're embarrassed that they've been "daydreaming."

I explain that their "daydreams" are more important than whatever I was saying. I encourage them to start observing where their mind wanders, instead of trying to control its movements, and I assure them that when they begin to take their daydreams seriously, they're likely to discover a rich source of remarkable information.

Marianne was amazed to discover that her unconscious mind could sneak its message into a seemingly irrelevant daydream. She'd come into therapy to deal with anxiety, which she blamed on stress at work. Although her conscious mind was clearly focused on her work situation as the source of her anxiety, I wondered if there wasn't another cause for Marianne's distress. She was engaged to be married, but she assured me that her relationship with her fiancé and her upcoming marriage were not the source of her problem.

During a session in which I was talking about the way the unconscious can unexpectedly supply us with information, I noticed that Marianne seemed self-absorbed. When I asked where she was, she blushed and apologized. She was very sorry, she said; she didn't mean to be rude, but her mind had just wandered away. At first she was reluctant to say what she was thinking about, then she said that it was silly, and she couldn't imagine what had made her think of it. *It* was a story she'd heard years before about a young couple who had married and were blissfully happy. On their first anniversary, however, the groom found his bride, dressed in her wedding dress, dead of an overdose of pills. Her suicide note said, "I'm sorry, I don't deserve to be this happy."

Marianne had had a very painful and cheerless childhood. She, too, was surprised by the joy and pleasure she was finally experiencing with her fiancé. She, too, questioned if she could renounce the *unhappy* cover her childhood had forced her to accept as the truth and allow herself to reach for the *joyful* under cover she had always hoped for, but never quite believed in. Now, when joy seemed within her grasp, she feared that the curse of her childhood would find a way to spoil everything. Consciously she discouraged these thoughts, but her unconscious found a way to get her attention, first by initiating anxiety, and then when she was in a safe place, by giving her a "wandering mind."

If you've always been vigilant or on guard, believing that you must watch out for whatever might go wrong, you've probably wasted a lot of your precious time and energy. If you're embarrassed when you do contradictory things or when your mind wanders, you don't understand that you are a multifaceted human being. You don't understand that your "I," your conscious mind, isn't all that you are. For just a moment accept your invisible ally and believe that you are not alone with your conscious resources. For the present you may find it too frightening or upsetting to accept that you are receiving help from an invisible source. Then, ask yourself what your life might be like if you could accept that fact. Life can be more balanced and harmonious when you learn to interpret the bulletins from your unconscious mind and get into the habit of trusting your intuitions.

WE ARE ALL WHAT WE ALL ARE

In desperate attempts to be who they think they *should* be, many people turn their backs on who they really are. They discount the information coming from themselves that threatens to expose their true selves. Day after day I see men and women who are ashamed of being shy, aggressive, sexy, or petty; people who blush and stammer when caught acting jealous, short tempered, or gullible, as though there were something wrong with being these things, as though these qualities were not in fact part of the human condition.

You can't be something that the rest of us are not. If something is true of you, it's true of us all. *It is not the characteristic but your need to deny it that is dangerous.* It's the suppression of a quality, not the quality itself, that harms you. Fear, grief, and even rage, will flare up and be gone, if they're fully expressed at the time they're experienced.

When you inhibit the expression of any trait, positive or negative, it hurts you. First, you must squander energy, hiding the hated quality. Second, even when you've successfully concealed it, you always suspect that, should this quality ever be exposed, it would cost you your place in another's affection. Third, unexpressed hidden emotions accumulated over time become a terrible psychic burden, which can cause internal damage.

Repression of qualities and emotions injures others as well. Unexpressed accumulated emotions can be indirectly expressed in seemingly innocuous ways, which can actually be hurtful. This is what is known as "passive aggression." When forced deeply under cover, accumulated emotions can sometimes erupt with really unpleasant consequences. We've all heard the stories about the man whom the neighbors vouch for as a "nice guy" who suddenly kills himself and his family.

It is the suppression over time that makes anger or despair break out in unmanageable and dangerous proportions. When you can recognize, accept, and express all of who you are, even those aspects of yourself that are not your favorites, you are less a danger to yourself or others. And you will have access to all of your energy, the energy you need to build your life.

Remember that you are receiving a steady stream of information coming from your unconscious mind; allow it to help you. By using slips of your tongue, causing you to forget to remember, encouraging your mind to wander, and in any number of other ways making you act like someone you don't recognize, your unconscious is teaching you about yourself. It is constantly telling you *who you are*, as well as stopping you from doing the things you're not yet ready to do. Let yourself listen and learn. The most important lessons you'll ever learn are those about yourself.

If even briefly you can put aside your old notion of who you *have to be*, and notice *what you actually do*, you may discover someone you didn't know was there. You may disapprove of some of the things you learn about yourself. Maybe you've always thought of yourself as, and always behaved like, a *generous* person. You might discover that you have a *stingy* streak. So what? Join the club.

When you see yourself behaving in contradictory ways, ways that challenge your idea of who you have to be, it may seem to your conscious mind that you're out of control. You may fear that your actions are random, unexplainable, and possibly even dangerous. But your unconscious mind is in control, and simply recognizing that your unconscious mind is in control can make a big difference in your life. In chapter 6, I introduce the cleverest of all the tricks in your unconscious's bag, that of "camouflage." It is your unconscious capacity to use camouflage—to direct your attention away from those things that endanger you—that is its most powerful method of keeping you from making changes prematurely. Recognizing and understanding this awesome maneuver can increase your appreciation of the silent guardian that vigilantly watches your back, jealously guards your darkest secrets, and will, the moment you are ready, return you to yourself.

Camouflage—
The Ultimate
Weapon of Your
Unconscious

Y our conscious mind is a scientist. With a logical, analytical, "just the facts, ma'am" approach to life, it urges you on, oblivious of danger. Your unconscious mind, on the other hand, is a magician. With flashing lights, disappearing tricks, and sleight of hand, it creates an obstacle course to distract you until it's safe for you to proceed.

Your unconscious comes to your rescue by using tactics that generally have a bad reputation. The master of disguise, distortion, and "what you see is not necessarily what you get," it steals your attention away from danger. The most ingenious technique at its disposal is "camouflage"—the trick of making something appear to be something it is not. If, in the previous chapter, you didn't recognize the way your unconscious protects you from change, you may discover it here.

Your unconscious may be directing your attention away from the change you want to make by creating a camouflage problem. It may use your body to camouflage dangerous emotions—hiding them in plain sight. Or, it may speak to you in your dreams, offering you camouflaged information in such a way as to give and withhold at the same time.

CAMOUFLAGE PROBLEMS

Perhaps you're standing at the growing edge facing a future danger, or the tip of the diving board facing a past danger. Your conscious mind may be yelling "Go ahead and jump!" But if you're not yet ready to risk the consequences of the leap, your unconscious may distract you by placing a camouflage problem between you and the chasm. This "problem" is compelling: you can't ignore it, but you also can't solve it, not until it's safe for you to jump.

REAL OR IMAGINED?

Identifying camouflage problems can be tricky. When I tell people that the problem they describe may be camouflage, they sometimes get angry. "It can't be camouflage," they say, "because it's real." It is not the nature—real or imagined—of the problem that makes it camouflage. It is the ability of this problem to sufficiently distract you from another change, one you're not yet ready to make, that qualifies it as camouflage.

Your unconscious can make literally anything compelling. Remember Joel, in the last chapter, who couldn't take his eyes off the tree outside my office window? Your unconscious can choose to use a "real" problem as your camouflage. It can take something that already concerns you and blow it out of proportion, as when some people are so worried about passing their exams that they can't concentrate on studying.

As camouflage, your unconscious can use problems you know you can't solve, but about which you nonetheless worry as if you *could* solve them. In this category we find worries about earthquakes and everyone else's problems.

108

Any concern, issue, or subject that is capable of capturing *your* attention can be *your* camouflage problem: anxiety about weight, work, love, health, or relationships; the desire to have a child; the ability to cook, dress, or understand computers—the variations are endless. Anything that gets your attention, anything that seems to you to be worth worrying about, can be a camouflage problem.

Something that seems insignificant to others can be a mighty camouflage problem to you. The only common thread in all camouflage problems is the capacity of the problem to compel and distract the person who has it.

Camouflage problems are designed to distract you from danger. With magical misdirection your unconscious focuses your attention on *a* problem that is not *the* problem. The following camouflage problems—weight, love, and work—are some of the most common camouflage problems in our culture.

WEIGHT

In our society, being overweight is a very common camouflage problem. Hundreds of thousands of people are obsessed with how much they weigh. An indication of how many people have camouflage weight problems is how the weight-loss business is booming. Dozens of new industries have sprung up to address this need. Where fad diets previously enjoyed fad popularity, weight loss programs have become a way of life for many people.

People for whom weight loss is a camouflage problem focus all their attention on it. Their lives revolve around their struggle to lose weight. They scrutinize their bodies, comparing themselves endlessly to everyone they encounter. They calculate calories, read diet books, enroll in weight-loss programs, sign up at health clubs, and buy expensive exercise equipment. Constantly evaluating their progress, even endlessly losing and gaining the same 5, 25, or 50 pounds, they diligently apply themselves to the problem, but they don't solve it. And that's what makes it a camouflage problem.

Does this sound familiar? Are you always worrying or talking about your weight? Do you spend much of your free time reading books about weight loss or related subjects? Are you weight-program literate, having tried every weight program on the market? Are food, exercise, and concealing clothing your favorite topics of conversation? When no matter what you do, you can't solve your problem, suspect camouflage. If your weight problem is a camouflage problem, its goal is to distract you, and by distracting you, protect you from a larger and more profound danger.

June came to see me to try to put an end to her lifelong struggle with her weight. June's parents were very religious and considered the human body sinful. At 35 years old June could still clearly remember one summer evening when she was only four. She'd found her mother's feather boa and, wearing only that and her birthday suit, paraded into the living room. Her parents blushed and awkwardly sent her to her room for punishment. June decided that her body, and her impulse to show it off, were shameful.

As she grew into a young woman, June's father called her friends who dated "tramps," and when June herself was finally allowed to date, she was admonished to "be careful." June was ashamed of her body. To hide it she created an *unattractive* cover and literally buried her body under cover, under layers of fat.

June may have buried her body under cover but she couldn't bury her sexuality, and even at her fattest she still attracted men. I asked June the What if? question. *What* would happen *if* she was thinner? After she explored the upside, the undeniable advantages to losing weight, June recognized her catastrophic expectation. "There would be no stopping me," she said. June believed that if she had a sexier body, she wouldn't be able to contain her sexuality, and her parents would despise her. The vision of her mother's tears and her father's red face were enough to undermine her most determined exercise program.

Before June can lose weight, she must feel safe enough to expose her sexuality. And before she can expose her sexuality, she must be able to disappoint her parents, to suffer their bad opinion of her. As long as this is too great a danger for June to face, her unconscious will keep her fascinated by all things related to weight loss—but it won't let her lose the weight.

WORK

Perhaps your camouflage problem is connected with work. In our society many people judge themselves and others by their jobs, believing that their personal worth is tied to their work. What they do, how much they do, how well they do it, and how much they're paid for it form the basis for their sense of self. For this reason, work and work-related issues are convincing camouflage problems for many.

Workaholism is an especially popular camouflage problem because it not only successfully distracts you from a larger danger, but has side benefits, such as material wealth and societal approval. Could workaholism be your camouflage? Have you been accused of being a workaholic? Do you proudly, self-righteously, or even grumpily proclaim that you "haven't had a vacation in months, years"? Do you keep planning to take time off, but somehow never can? Do you spend all your free time thinking or worrying about the success of your business? If you're employed by someone else, do you worry obsessively about your status at work, who has which office or parking space, who will get the big promotion, or who is your boss's favorite? Do you take work home, imagine yourself to be indispensable, or worry about the business as if it were your own?

You don't have to like your job, in fact you don't even have to *have* a job, for work to function as your camouflage problem. You can be a perpetual student, worry about getting a job you like, complain about how much you hate your job, or spend years trying to figure out the career that's right for you. If you

111

pass a lot of your time focusing on work or work-related problems that you never seem to solve, work may be your camouflage.

Leona came to see me because she wanted to expand her business, but she couldn't seem to do it. As a teenager she'd turned the family basement into a factory where she'd designed, manufactured, and distributed a line of picture frames. But at 25, she was still working in her parents' basement and living in her parents' home. She wanted to expand—to hire a salesperson and move to larger quarters—but she couldn't make herself do it.

I asked Leona the What if? question: What would happen if she expanded her business? When she expanded her business, she said, she'd make more money, feel good about herself, and be happier. Then, as an afterthought, Leona added that she might move out of her parents' house.

When I asked what would happen if she moved out of her parents' home, Leona said, "Who'll pick up Grandma, or go to the grocery store?" Leona knew her parents could do these things for themselves, but she couldn't quite shake the feeling that she shouldn't leave.

Leona was the younger of two children. At 15, her older sister, Maggie, ran away from home, which Leona believed "devastated" her parents. Leona adopted a *good* cover to balance Maggie's *bad* cover. Although not consciously aware of it, Leona equated leaving home with abandoning and devastating her parents, something she decided at an early age she would never do.

To protect her parents, Leona had put her life on hold. Her apathy was a perfect camouflage. As long as she couldn't expand her business, she couldn't leave.

The change Leona really needed to make was to separate from her parents. I encouraged her to stop thinking about the business for a short while and focus on her life. Leona has started to date, and now has a steady boyfriend. Although she's not thinking much about it, Leona has begun the separation process. And the expansion of her business, which was a camouflage problem, just doesn't seem so important anymore.

If you're spending endless hours worrying about quitting your job, starting a business, selling your business, telling off your boss, firing your assistant, getting promoted, or showing up a co-worker—maybe work is your camouflage.

LOVE

Wanting to be loved is perhaps the most common camouflage problem in our society. When Linda Ronstadt sang "When Will I Be Loved?" she spoke to the concerns of hundreds of thousands of people. Do you believe that your happiness depends on your being loved by someone else? Do you spend much of your time worrying that you're not loved, or not loved well enough? Do you judge everything in your life on the basis of its ability to make you more lovable, or bring love into your life? If so, you fit the profile of a person for whom love is a camouflage problem.

The desire to be loved is compelling camouflage, but so is the desire to be the perfect lover. Are you constantly worrying about a loved one—parent, spouse, or child? Do you find it difficult to let other people solve their own problems? Do your interchanges with others often involve someone's being lectured, corrected, or fixed? When other people's problems distract you from, or even take precedence over, your own problems, love—or the co-dependent caretaking that is sometimes confused with love—is your camouflage.

As with weight loss, "co-dependence"—which is putting another's well-being before your own, to the detriment of both—has spawned an industry. As with weight loss, the problem is very real. Hundreds of thousands of people are addicted to a loved one and unable to see past their loved one's

113

need: a son's bad marriage, a daughter's inability to find a man, a husband's drinking problem, a sister's critical boss, a teenage child's fight with her boyfriend or his girlfriend. When co-dependence is your camouflage, there's no shortage of people to co-depend on.

Couples can provide an unending supply of camouflage distractions for each other. Concentrating on how the other is wrong, bad, sick, hurtful, or in danger, they never have to think about their own problems.

Ironically, the quality we're trying to correct in the other is often the very quality we deny in ourselves, the one we've kept under cover. And as long as we must continue to disown it, focusing on how the other person should change can provide an excellent camouflage. Faith and Darrell had only been married a year when they came into therapy. Neither wanted to be there but they didn't know what else to do. What had been an exciting love affair was rapidly becoming a slugfest.

As the strictly brought-up oldest child of a deeply religious family, Faith had an *I'm good* cover. As the overindulged baby boy of a show-biz family, Darrell had an *I'm bad* cover. These differences, which had attracted them to each other, both needing to reclaim the denied under cover so perfectly represented by the other, were now tearing them apart.

Instead of learning from each other how to use these qualities, they immediately began trying to get the other one to change. It began with good-natured teasing. She called him her "bad boy" and tried to get him to "grow up." He called her "little Miss Manners" and encouraged her to "let her hair down." By the time they came to see me, she was accusing him of being a "criminal" and he was calling her a "Nazi." The dramatic escalation of their name calling suggested just how terrified each was of accepting his or her "dreadful" under cover.

Both of them needed to unbalance their family by reclaiming their denied qualities, but neither was ready to do that, so for each the other's intransigence became the perfect camouflage.

In therapy they explored the messages they'd received from their families that caused them to adopt their covers. I encouraged them to risk exposing their under covers by acting in the "awful" way the other did. Could he, for example, be overly polite when they went out with friends? Could she put off returning phone calls and forget to send thank-you notes once in a while?

Darrell and Faith are trying, but it's very difficult for them. Exposing their secret selves will badly disappoint their families. She will have to admit she's not as *good* as her religious family believes her to be, and he will have to admit that he's more *conventional* than his family raised him to be. As long as they can't renounce their covers, their attempts to change each other provide them with camouflage, an efficient distraction from their own dangerous changes.

What are you most annoyed by or worried about? What do you often complain about? What do you wish you could stop thinking about? What are other people tired of hearing you bring up? The answers to these questions can provide clues to your camouflage problem. You may not be able to identify your camouflage problem until you're ready to face your larger danger. But when you're ready to confront your larger danger, your camouflage problem will probably be easily solved, and not seem quite so important.

IN THE MEANWHILE

Camouflage problems can be real problems that you care deeply about, but cannot solve. When people in therapy recognize that a problem that has been "driving them crazy" is actually camouflage, and, as such, is insolvable for the present, they sometimes get discouraged and sarcastically say, "Great, so what do I do now?"

I tell them that recognizing their struggle with weight, work, or love to be camouflage can free them to use the time, energy, and creativity they've been squandering on attempts to solve the insolvable on enjoying themselves. I tell them that if they can't, for the moment, solve their problem, they might as well spend some of the time in pleasurable pursuits.

If you begin to suspect that a problem that's been driving you "crazy" is actually a camouflage problem, try giving yourself a rest. Is there someone that you'd really like to see or talk to? Go ahead and call them. Do you love to walk on the beach or play tennis? Take a break and treat yourself. Does a massage, a pedicure, or cup of tea sound good to you? You don't have to forget all about the problem, just put it aside, on the back burner, for the time being. If it's camouflage, you can't do anything about it now; and if it isn't camouflage, it will still be there when you get back.

OTHER KINDS OF CAMOUFLAGE

As I said at the beginning of this chapter, there are many ways in which your unconscious uses camouflage. The first is the camouflage problem. The second is by enlisting your body in the attempt to disguise a danger you aren't ready to tackle. If you don't recognize any of the camouflage problems, perhaps your unconscious has chosen to use its favorite accomplice to protect you from yourself—your body.

THE MIND/BODY CONNECTION

Just as it does with the Freudian slip, your unconscious can use your body to send you important information. It can manipulate

116

your body to stop you from doing things that your conscious mind doesn't recognize as dangerous. In his book *Love and Will*, psychotherapist Rollo May describes a distraught patient who came to him suffering from impotence. This man did not want to be impotent. Why, then, did his unconscious stop his body from working? Dr. May tells us that the man's wife would "take off her shoe while they were driving and beat him over the head with it." He concludes: "By all means the man was impotent in this hideous caricature of a marriage. And his penis . . . seemed to be the only character with enough "sense" to have the appropriate intention, namely to get out as quickly as possible."

Your unconscious is constantly using your body to give you all kinds of information. In the case of Dr. May's patient, his body volunteered its information; it acted. But as Larry discovered, you sometimes have to ask for it. Larry came to see me to stop being so accommodating. Although co-owner of his retail business, he did most of the drudge work. One of his goals in therapy was to start "acting like the boss."

Larry had been invited to go skiing on the upcoming Presidents' Day holiday, but thought he should work. When I asked him what he *wanted* to do, he said he "didn't know." I told Larry that a part of him probably did know what he wanted to do, but another part thought it wasn't safe for him to recognize it. I asked Larry to repeat two sentences: "I *do* want to work on Presidents' Day," and "I *don't* want to work on Presidents' Day." He easily repeated the first, but his "mouth didn't want to say the second." Saying "I *don't* want . . ." might expose the *don't push me around* under cover he'd spent his life denying.

Larry's conscious mind wanted him to "stop being a push-over." It didn't understand that perpetuating his *accommodating* cover was protecting him from the danger of having to confront his past. Larry was startled to see that his mouth had a mind of it's own. It was only when his mouth resisted speaking the words "I don't want . . ." that Larry was able to consider that there might be a good reason for his accommodating behavior. It was at this point that therapy could actually begin, because it was at this point that the *real* problem—his childhood decision to accommodate a domineering father—could begin to be explored.

In therapy, when someone tells me that they don't know what they want, I invite them to ask their mouth. I suggest that they say out loud, "I want this," and "I don't want that." It's remarkable how often your mouth, through its reluctance to say one of these phrases, can give you, in an instant, an answer that your conscious mind, with all its logical skills, could not provide.

Larry had to *ask* his mouth for the information he wanted. But Kathy's body was constantly offering her information that, because she didn't understand it, she disregarded. Kathy was a gentle, softspoken young woman who had a history of unexplained headaches. While not incapacitating, they were very unpleasant. Because her conscious mind never recognized the very definite pattern of these headaches, she thought of them as an annoying, inexplicable fact of her life.

As a child, whenever Kathy said "No," or "I don't want to," her mother put on a sad face and withdrew emotionally. Her mother's withdrawal was too big a price for Kathy to pay for disagreement, and saying no became a danger she avoided at all costs. When Kathy really didn't want to do something, her unconscious and her body came to her rescue by creating a headache. She had an ironclad excuse for saying no because she couldn't help it if she had a headache, could she?

Until she could risk facing the danger of facing a loved one's disapproval, Kathy's conscious mind couldn't see the connection between saying no and her headaches. In therapy she was exploring the possibility that she could endure the withdrawal of affection. She realized that when she could risk this withdrawal she would no longer need to blame her headache when she said no. Then she would no longer need her headaches.

One night Kathy had dinner with her boyfriend, Andre. When he said he wanted to spend the night, she began to get a headache, which worsened as they drove home. When they got to her door, she took a very big risk. Although it was difficult for her, she took a deep breath and said she was tired and wanted to call it a night. Andre went home by himself, and in a short time Kathy's headache disappeared.

The unconscious commonly uses several parts of the body to get our attention. Just about everyone has had a "tension headache" or a "nervous stomach." You may never have consciously understood that these are messages from your unconscious, but that is nonetheless what they often are. The unconscious frequently uses the neck and shoulders, stomach, or jaw to carry its information. But again, this is "person specific." I know a singer who carries her distress in her throat, and an artist who feels his anxiety in his hands. If your unconscious is using your body to talk to you, the message is always there.

Do you know how your unconscious conspires with your body to protect you from a danger you may not even see and how it stops you from doing things your conscious "wants" to do? Ask yourself the following questions:

- Do you always get a toothache when you have to see your brother-in-law?
- Do you have trouble staying awake through a particular class?
- Is there a special pain in your toe or upper arm that you only experience when you go shopping with your wife?
- Do you get that "sinking feeling" in the pit of your stomach whenever you're anxious or frightened?
- Is a headache a sure sign that you should be, but aren't, crying?

You may not know how to read your "body language," but you can learn. Listen to your body over time, especially in moments of stress, because it's never too late to begin the study.

THE BODY—A STOREHOUSE OF FEELINGS. Dangerous feelings and painful memories that must be hidden from your conscious mind can be placed by your unconscious mind in your body for safekeeping. There it can hide these dangerous secrets by converting them into physical sensations. Thoughts, feelings, and memories turn into headaches, backaches, stomachaches; a tightening of the shoulders, neck, or jaw muscles; a tingly feeling in the arms or legs; or a numbness of entire sections of the body. Once the conversion is complete, even you believe that you don't have those thoughts, feelings, or memories—only the physical sensation.

Stephanie came into therapy on the recommendation of her physical therapist because her back and neck pain were not responding to treatment. At 23 she was a small, polite, perfectly controlled young woman. When I asked her if anything besides her neck was bothering her, she said that her family had forbidden her to see her boyfriend. When I asked her how she felt about that she looked puzzled. "I don't feel anything," she said, "I just sort of go numb."

Stephanie's family had emigrated from a war-torn country. Before she was ten, Stephanie had witnessed several brutal murders. When I asked her to close her eyes and concentrate on the pain in her neck, she saw "a room with white walls, all splattered with blood."

Stephanie had been a helpless, terrified little girl in a hazardous environment. To protect her from her terror, Stephanie's unconscious buried her fear in her neck and shoulders. Feelings of any kind threatened to expose Stephanie's buried terror, so she adopted an *I don't feel, I go numb* cover.

Until it is safe enough for Stephanie to reexperience her terror, it's unlikely that the pain in her neck will respond, except temporarily, to the physical therapy she's receiving.

It isn't only terrifying or traumatic events that we must conceal but also normal thoughts and feelings we can't safely express. As children we don't want to be angry, or sad, or scared, or even happy, if the expression of these feelings displeases our parents. Once we've established our cover, the under cover qualities that don't fit with the image must be split off and hidden from the world—and ourselves.

When you're first learning how to hide the thoughts, feelings, and qualities that might cause trouble, you pretend they're not happening. "No, Mommy," you say, "I'm not sad." After a while you become an accomplished little actor and are quite convincing. Finally, your unconscious finds a way to bury this information from even your conscious mind, and you grow up thinking of yourself as someone who's never sad. You *are* the happy little boy or girl your parents wanted you to be. You become your cover.

Christine came into therapy because she was depressed. When she talked about how her husband criticized and humiliated her in public, she had a big smile on her face. When I commented that her smile seemed incongruous with the story she was telling, Christine's face crumbled and she started to cry. Then she recalled a memory from her childhood.

When she was six years old, her older brother, Tom, accidentally broke her toy. When she started to cry, Tom said, "Don't cry, Chrissy—remember how upset Mommy was when Sue had her nervous breakdown? Mom can't stand it if you're sad, too. You have to be happy."

Christine was the baby girl. Adored from birth, she was assigned a *happy* cover; she certainly didn't want to upset her mother. She couldn't stop the sad feelings from coming, but she could stop them from showing. At first she simply pretended not to be sad, but soon her unconscious took over. Every time Christine felt sad, every time she was in danger of disappointing her mother, Christine's unconscious put a big smile on her face. This was repeated over and over until the two events—the sadness and the smile—were linked together. Although her conscious mind had no awareness of it, sadness *made* Christine smile.

Your unconscious mind knows where all your secret thoughts, feelings, and memories are hidden, because it put them there. As long as the information being stored in your body is too painful or frightening for you to deal with, your unconscious will keep it hidden. It's a very effective technique but only useful as a temporary measure. After a while the body begins to pay a price for carrying a burden it wasn't really designed to bear.

While it's keeping your dangerous secrets, your unconscious is also keeping a record of every time the conversion from feeling to physical sensation takes place inside you. When you're ready to face a danger you've been avoiding, your unconscious can show you these recordings.

EXERCISE—*The Body Video*

Have you begun to recognize where your unconscious is putting information in your body? Have you identified your "storehouse"? If so, then pay close attention to the aches, pains, or tingles you feel there. You can learn a lot about the danger from which your unconscious is protecting you by listening to your body.

In the past when you've had these sensations you may have tried to shift your attention, ignore the feeling, or even make it go away. Now when you notice one of these sensations, you might want to try the following exercise, which appeals directly to the part of your body feeling the sensation and holding the information:

Close your eyes to eliminate distractions, locate the sensation in your body, and focus your attention on it. If you're tempted to try to make it go away, notice your resistance. Your resistance may come in the form of a different physical sensation. You may have an urge to scratch your nose, or feel a tingling in your fingertips. If this is so, focus on the new sensation. Take whatever your body offers you. Having settled on the sensation, encourage it to expand—to escalate and become as large as it possibly can. If you feel frightened, remind yourself that your unconscious will only give you information you can use, and will not allow you to stray into territory that is too dangerous.

Take time just to observe. Where exactly is the sensation located? How far does it extend? How big can you get it to be? Is it familiar? Is it an ache, a pain, a pang, or something for which you have no word? Do you associate this physical sensation with an emotion? Is it sadness, rage, fear?

While you're concentrating on the sensation, speak directly to the part of your body that is feeling it. In your imagination say, "Thank you, stomach, for taking over these painful feelings for me. I know you've done this to protect me. I know you've kept a record of each time you've done it, including the very first time. If I'm ready to see it now, please find some way to show it to me."

You may get no new information, finding instead that you're hungry, sleepy, thinking about something you've forgotten to do, or bored and annoyed by the whole exercise. Whatever you experience, you're getting exactly what your unconscious believes you can handle.

And you may receive a lot of information. Your unconscious is amazingly inventive and will use a variety of methods to show you what it wants you to know. This information can come as a thought or a memory. You may see a replay of the event that started it all. You may hear a song or see a photograph. You may see a cartoon or a series of quick pictures in which nothing really stands out. You may experience contrasting emotions: if you're angry, you may feel sad. You may experience contrasting physical sensations. You may see animals, colors, or a toy you had as a child. You may find yourself in the house of your childhood, some other significant place, or a place that you've never seen before. The information may come all in a rush, or in pieces over time.

You may "see" a series of scenes from your own life, scenes that have a theme or a common thread. Perhaps in every one you are sad, or feel threatened. Maybe you're angry but not letting on; maybe you're embarrassed or feel cheated. And every time you had that experience you also had the same pain, ache, or tingle in the same part of your body. Every time your unconscious converted the feeling and the memory of the event into a physical sensation, it kept a silent record.

You may be wondering what use you can make of the information you obtain in this way. Well, look at how Shirley, in the following example, used what she learned about herself from her stomach.

Shirley was sure she no longer wanted an exclusive relationship with Mark. She knew that he wasn't the right man for her, so she couldn't understand why whenever she saw him, she had to resist the impulse to ask him to come back.

Whenever Shirley talked about turning her back on Mark she was aware of a "scared feeling in the pit of her stomach." I suggested that she concentrate on this feeling and ask it for help. When she did, she saw a series of "snapshots."

"I saw myself coming home from school and my parents saying that my kitten died," she said. "I saw the six or eight different homes we lived in when I was a kid, and some of the friends I never saw again. I saw my mom crying and saying that Grammy died. I saw my dad leaving when my parents got divorced."

Shirley's early life was filled with losses. As a child she'd wondered why she lost everyone she loved and who she would lose next. What would happen to her? Who would take care of her, and what was wrong with her? The adults around her, consumed by their own pain and blind to hers, couldn't answer these questions. No one comforted or reassured her.

Shirley was overwhelmed by feelings. To protect her, her unconscious stored these feelings and the memories that went with them in the pit of her stomach, and Shirley adopted an *I lose everything I love* cover.

Loss of any kind, even one that was "good for her," one she'd chosen and orchestrated for herself, provoked those early memories and feelings. When she saw Mark leaving, Shirley's stomach remembered all of her losses and she got scared.

Although she was sure she didn't want to be with Mark, Shirley had assumed that the fear she felt as she watched him leave meant she didn't *want* him to leave. Realizing that it was loss itself that made her feel so bad, not the particular loss of Mark, allowed her finally to detach from him. Since loss of any kind terrified Shirley, she had a history of holding on to things and people long after she wanted them. Now that she understood what her stomach was telling her, she found that it was much easier for her to "let go."

DREAMS

Your unconscious may be using your body to camouflage dangerous feelings or memories. Another place the unconscious uses its camouflage tricks is in our dreams. Although difficult to interpret, dreams can be a source of important information about the dangers that block change.

Dreams are the natural territory of the unconscious and one of its most powerful methods of communication. Watching the nightly late show in your mind can introduce you to aspects of yourself you've forgotten, denied, or never gotten to know very well. Your dreams can dramatically present the conflicts of your past and the struggles of your present. They can post detour signs to help you avoid danger. But like the Freudian slip or the mixed message, the information in your dreams can be difficult to decipher. You simultaneously understand, and are confused by, the message.

Even when we don't understand our dreams, they fascinate us. "I had the most amazing dream last night," we say. "I was flying," "I was drowning," "I was making love," "It was so real."

We can wake from our dreams reluctant to leave them or anxious to put them behind us. Whether you're aware of dreaming every night, or believe that you never dream, your dreams are an entry point to your unconscious mind. The more seriously you take them, the more you can benefit from them.

Many cultures have respected dreams and dreaming. The Senoi Indians begin each day by recounting their dreams to family members and using the information they receive to plan their lives. Shakespeare believed that dreams ". . . knit up the raveled sleeve of care." Philosophers, writers, scientists, and psychological theorists have all speculated on their purpose. Are they a rehash of the day's events? Do they foretell the future? Are they just "a bit of undigested meat," as Scrooge hoped the apparition of Jacob Marley would turn out to be? Or are they "just a dream" with no significance at all?

Many techniques have been devised for understanding the language of dreams, and every psychological theory has one. Freud called dreams the "royal road to the unconscious," and prescribed free association. Jung, to whom dreams were "a little hidden door in the innermost and most secret recesses of the soul," suggested writing poems and stories or making drawings based on the dream.

Gestalt theorists say that each dream is a snapshot of the ego in which the "you" in your dream represents the parts of yourself you accept—your cover—and everything else in the dream represents the parts of yourself you deny—your under cover. They suggest role playing or "dialoguing" with the denied parts. All seem to agree with Jung that "no dream symbol can be separated from the individual who dreams it." In other words, the final judge of what your dream means is—you.

126

The research shows that, whether they know it or not, everyone dreams every night. Even people who swear that they never dream often remember one significant dream from their childhood, recall an occasional dream, or are now and then visited by a series of dreams. You may not understand your dreams; you may not even believe that you dream; but when you're in the middle of a problem or a crisis, your unconscious will often send you a dream that somehow seems important.

Charles came into therapy to stop feeling scared in relationships. Whenever he was in an important relationship, no matter how well it seemed to be going, he felt certain he'd be *abandoned*. Charles's parents seemed loving and accepting of him, and he had no memory of any childhood trauma to account for his *abandonment* cover. During the course of therapy, Charles had a dream.

> I'm two years old and in the backseat of a car. My parents are in the front seat. I can see danger approaching from the rear, but my parents don't see it. I'm trying to warn them of the danger but I can't get their attention. Finally, my parents see the danger and we rush out of the car. We back up against a wall to avoid the oncoming danger. Suddenly, the wall seems to swallow my mother, leaving me alone with my father.

Charles was very disturbed by this dream. He thought it meant that he'd been abandoned by his mother. He questioned his parents closely about his early childhood and discovered that his mother had been very sick and hospitalized for a short time several months after he was born.

Bringing this event to his conscious awareness confirmed for Charles that he had a good reason for feeling *abandoned*. It put an end to his civil war, in which he was constantly accusing himself of being crazy for feeling abandoned. Once he put his fear of loss in its proper perspective, he felt more trusting and less fearful in his current relationships.

It may not even be necessary to interpret your dream. Sometimes simply having—and accepting—it is enough to make you feel better. Sylvia had been anxious for days, although she didn't know why. When she woke from the following dream, she found the anxiety had gone.

> I'm swimming laps in my pool. I'm swimming in my regular lane at my regular pace, but the pool is unusually long, "and seems to go on forever." I'm delighted to notice that the pool is filled with all kinds of vividly colored and variously shaped fish. Then, I see that there are sharks swimming near the bottom of the pool. "Oh well," I think to myself, "sharks will stay at the bottom, unless you disturb them." And with that thought I go on happily doing my laps.

Sylvia decided that with this dream her unconscious mind was telling her to "let sleeping dogs (sharks) lie"—that whatever conflict she might have to face in the future could wait. Sylvia was happy to accept this decision.

When your unconscious wants you to know something, it can speak to you directly in a dream. It can put the words it wants you to hear in someone else's mouth, or it can have the *you* in your dream deliver the important speech. It can have you dream of a neon sign, a billboard, or a person with a placard. Your unconscious can use puns to communicate. Lisa was having second thoughts about telling her father about the effect his cold and distant manner had on her self-esteem. Then she dreamed that she'd "gone into the kitchen and found something that I'd left cooking on the back burner, which needed my attention before it burned." Having this dream reassured Lisa that her decision to confront her father was the right one, and she proceeded to do so.

When trying to understand a dream, you must sometimes suspend judgment. The apparent message isn't always the correct one. Your dream may be giving you a chance to peek at your under cover. It may be showing you things about yourself that are unknown to your conscious mind.

Your unconscious often uses dreams to demonstrate aspects of yourself that you've had to deny. If some of the characters in your dreams seem scary or bad, consider the possibility that they represent an under cover quality. Perhaps the only reason the quality appears bad to you is that your family would disapprove if you displayed it, and you still need to protect yourself and them by denying the quality.

When you're ready to reclaim an under cover quality, your unconscious may use your dreams to prepare you for its reappearance. You may dream that you or others behave uncharacteristically. You may dream that you're being given a gift or an award.

Dreams of integration may have you finding or discovering things that you'd lost or mislaid. Lionel is a librarian, and shortly before deciding to stop therapy he had this dream.

> I was wandering around in the stacks when I came upon a suitcase hidden behind the shelves. I realized that this was my suitcase, filled with my things that I'd left there long ago for safekeeping and somehow forgotten all about until now. I was very happy to have it back.

Dreams that symbolize the reclaiming of a quality belonging to the opposite-sex parent can sometimes have you finding or even stealing objects. Stacy and Maureen were both trying to become more aggressive in their workplace, a quality that had belonged to their fathers. Stacy dreamed that she was stealing her father's pen, and Maureen dreamed that she'd found and kept a man's attaché case, because it contained things she expected to need.

Lovemaking in dreams can represent the integration of previously denied qualities. Heterosexual men and women are sometimes uncomfortable with dreams of lovemaking with a same-sex partner, but these dreams may have nothing to do with your sexual preference. They may instead signal your readiness to reclaim an under cover quality that belonged to a same-sex parent you antimodeled as a child.

If you're interested in your dreams, what they mean, and how to get in closer touch with them, there are many wonderful books on the subject, and many therapists who specialize in helping people understand their dreams. There are also dream groups consisting of people who, like the Senoi, share their dreams and help each other learn from them.

Writers, artists, philosophers, inventors, and scientists have all reported receiving information and inspiration from their dreams. Some say that a vital part of their work came to them in a dream. Remembering your dreams, writing them down, playing with them, and sharing them with friends or loved ones can provide surprising insights and information.

POWERBOAT VS. SAILBOAT

The conscious mind is like a powerboat. Once it's decided on a destination, it heads straight for it, choosing the shortest distance between two points. The unconscious is like a sailboat. Even with a chosen destination it cannot head into the wind. It must often "tack," or go in the opposite direction from its destination in order to get into position to approach that destination safely.

It may seem to you that your unconscious is devious, but this subterfuge can be necessary if your conscious mind, mistakenly believing that it "knows" all there is to know, is stubbornly urging you toward a danger it doesn't see.

Your unconscious may well be stopping you from doing some of the things you want to do. It may seem to be piloting you in the opposite direction from where you want to go, but it isn't. By maneuvering you, tinkering with the things you say, do, think, and remember, by distracting you with camouflage problems, hiding dangerous feelings in your body and sending you cryptic messages in your dreams, your unconscious is protecting you from the rocky reefs you may not see.

Until you recognize the benevolent intentions of your unconscious mind, your conscious mind may be indicting you for not changing. In the next chapter I talk about how we condemn ourselves for feeling bad and pretend to be "normal." I also catalog the most popular methods we use when trying to force ourselves into change.

The Things
We Do for Change

I f you can't do what you want to do, there's a very good reason why you can't. But to discover your reason, you must discover yourself. Are lessons learned from your family stopping you from becoming who you want to be? Will the change you want to make bring you face-to-face with a future or past danger? To find the answer you must investigate your own history; you must look into your own heart.

Until you can do the kind of archaeological research that will bring your secrets to light, that will make it possible for you to risk your change, your unconscious mind will distract and protect you. And just as soon as you can survive that exposure your unconscious will aid you in wonderfully unexpected ways.

I hope you're beginning to think differently about the trouble you're having making the change you want to make. I hope that rather than thinking there's something wrong with you because you can't change, or criticizing yourself for not changing, you're beginning to wonder *why* you can't change. It's time to ask yourself some of the following questions:

- In what way will making this change upset the balance of my family, blow my cover, expose an under cover, or rock a relationship boat?

133

- What danger or catastrophic expectations do I anticipate when I make this change?
- What emotions or unpleasant memories may be triggered by this change?
- How have I used my difficulty making this change as ammunition against myself in my very own private civil war?
- How has my unconscious mind stopped me from making this change? Which of its tricks has it used to protect me?
- What camouflage problem has kept me busy and distracted me from the larger danger I may not yet be ready to face?
- What can I learn from my body and my dreams that will help me understand the difficulty I'm having?

When you ask yourself these questions, instead of "What am I doing wrong?" and "How can I fix it?" you shift your focus from trying to be who you think you ought to be, to allowing yourself to be who you *are*.

FEELING BAD ABOUT
FEELING BAD

There's a myth in our culture—which is hard to understand, with so many people in therapy—that "good," "smart," or "healthy" people don't feel bad. If you're in emotional pain, this myth seems to say, there's something wrong with you. If you're in therapy, it hints, you must have done something wrong. Consequently, I am often asked by anxious clients if what they're doing, thinking, feeling, experiencing, or wishing for is normal. Timidly they ask, "Am I neurotic?" "Have you ever seen this before?" "Does anyone else act, feel, or think this way?" In addition to the anguish they feel over their problems, they suffer the shame of thinking that because they hurt, they are somehow abnormal, wrong, or bad.

When I first started to practice psychotherapy I was startled by how many people asked me if they were "normal." I expected people to ask "How did I get this way?" and "What can I do about it?" and even "How long will it take to fix?" But I didn't anticipate the overwhelming concern so many people have about being "normal."

If you believe this myth—if you're ashamed that you can't do something you want to do, and you worry that it means there's something wrong with you—relax. Aside from the fact that you hurt, there's nothing wrong with you. You didn't do anything wrong. You're no doubt reacting, as anyone would, to the circumstances of your life. Anyone who had your history would be likely to think, feel, hurt, and experience the world exactly as you do. But even if no one else in the world is hurting precisely the way you're hurting, you don't deserve to hurt and you *do* deserve to feel better.

You don't have to feel bad about feeling bad—and the first step you can take toward feeling better is to stop your civil war. Interrupt your critical inner dialogue and replace it with some sweet talk. Send yourself comforting messages—messages that support you in your struggle, that contain kindness, acceptance, and encouragement. Tell yourself that you didn't do anything wrong and you're doing the best you can—because that's really the truth. Remember that the world is more than willing to criticize, judge, and even scorn you. You need and deserve an advocate. Trust that you won't "take advantage" of the kindness you offer yourself. Give yourself a break.

YOU–NIQUE

Our society is obsessed with normality. If a thing is "normal"— the way other people experience it—even if it doesn't fit you, it's acceptable. If you don't find yourself reflected in the sitcoms, movies, or popular songs, you may worry that you're somehow wrong or abnormal. If your pain isn't a popular pain, you may feel ashamed and keep your difference a secret. If your struggle isn't a widespread struggle, you may deny it. But the popularity of your suffering doesn't define it's normality or dictate your right to take it seriously.

It took Rock Hudson's admission that he had AIDS to get the disease media attention and Magic Johnson's admission of HIV infection to give it urgency, but the media coverage that AIDS has received is not what makes it a serious problem. Anita Hill's testimony that she'd been sexually harassed by her employer, Clarence Thomas, gave thousands of women the courage to talk about their experiences, but did not create the problem of harassment. When several well-known personalities courageously spoke up about their childhood molestation, thousands of "regular folk" who had previously suffered in silence were finally able to come for help. When these celebrities went "public," many who also struggled with these painful conditions finally felt safe enough to admit it.

Every day, someone shyly and shamefacedly confides to me and other therapists, as though confessing to a crime, that he or she is impulsive, compulsive, agoraphobic, anorexic, or bulimic; a victim of incest, an insomniac, secretly homo-, bi-, or asexual; addicted to drugs, alcohol, food, work, or sex; unable to reach orgasm, remember their childhood, or love their parents; passive, aggressive, painfully shy, lonely, or afraid of the dark.

These are not crimes. When you can't make yourself do something, or make yourself stop doing something, there is a *very good reason.* Don't add the shame of self-condemnation to the pain caused by the problem.

What society considers right, proper, correct, or normal changes, and sometimes very quickly. The foods I was encouraged to eat as a child, I am now encouraged to avoid.

The sexual mores taught in the '50s disappeared in the '60s, but seem to have returned again in the '90s. In the space of six months the Russians went from being our enemy to being a victim in need of our help, and Robert Gates had trouble getting confirmed as the head of the CIA because he was too anti-Russian, the very qualification that had won him the job in the first place.

In his movie *Sleeper*, Woody Allen spoofs this tendency of society to change its mind about what is good, bad, right, or wrong. In it he wakes to a future where junk-food stores have replaced health-food stores and everyone is trying to consume as much sugar and fat as they can.

The rules will change. We can't count on what is thought to be "right" or "normal" today being so thought of tomorrow. Do you want to make your particular change because it's the "correct" or the "normal" thing to do? If so, take a moment to ask yourself if this change really fits *you*. If you're trying to make this change in order to fit into society's definition of "normal," you probably won't succeed. Trying to fit in, or conform to someone else's idea of "normal," wastes your time and derails your search for the real you. Trying to be someone you're not is like trying to swim against the current; you may travel a short distance, but it's such hard work and you'll just fall back eventually.

WHO ARE YOU?

If the change you want to make requires you to be someone you're not—if you want to be a surgeon, for example, but the sight of blood makes you faint—no amount of wanting or trying will make you able to do it. If the change you want to make violates a cover story you've spent your life pretending was the truth—you have a high IQ but your family balance demands that you act *dumb*—making this change may unbalance your family. The more clearly you can identify *who you are* as opposed to *who you believe you ought to be*, the more clearly you will understand the obstacles in your path to change.

Instead of looking outward to find out who you are, look inward. The answers *are* there. Don't be afraid; there is no right or wrong, there is only who you are. While we human beings are all basically the same, the variety of ways to be human is endless. Some of the following questions may help you begin to know yourself better.

- Who are your favorite fictional characters?
- Are you a saver or a spender?
- Who are your favorite historical figures?
- Are you a joiner or a loner?
- Whom do you identify with in the movies?
- Are you a daytime or a nighttime person?
- What was your favorite childhood fairy tale?
- Are you punctual or tardy?
- What did you want to be when you grew up?
- Are you sloppy or neat?

While you were asking yourself these questions or even just reading the list, did you find yourself judging one or another or the characteristics suggested there? Did you think to yourself, "Boy I'm glad that's not me," or "Yuck, that's true of me"? Do you know where you got the idea that a certain quality was "bad"? Is there anyone that you admire despite the fact that they demonstrate this "bad" quality? Besides yourself, who would really be upset to discover that *you* possessed this "bad" quality? Don't be concerned if you can't answer all of these questions; "knowing thyself" is a worthy goal, but it takes time.

THE "RIGHT" VS. THE "WRONG" WAY

Believing that there's a right way to do things may well keep you from finding your way to do them. Hoagy Carmichael, the composer of "Deep Purple" and "Stardust," ignored his song ideas because he thought he wasn't a "good enough piano player to be a composer." One night at a party he heard Irving Berlin playing the piano. Hoagy realized that he could "play better than Irving," and began composing immediately. Hoagy Carmicheal was always a composer—only *he* didn't know it. His idea of what he had to be before he could compose music was wrong.

USING WHAT YOU HAVE

There's more than one way to do everything, and *your* way, although different from others, can still be the right way. You have your own strengths, abilities, and ways of doing things. For just a moment stop wishing you were something you're not and try to appreciate who you are. The more you understand who *you* are, the more you can benefit from what *you* can do, which may be very special. Brian is a screenwriter whose path to success is unusual. Brian is functionally illiterate; he can't write a complete sentence. He was sure he had good story ideas, but he couldn't put those ideas down on paper. Instead of trying to get himself to function the way other screenwriters do, Brian used a special talent. He visualized his stories in exacting detail. He "daydreamed" his stories until he could see the entire screenplay from start to finish. Then, as he "watched the movie in his head," Brian dictated what he saw into a tape recorder. He gave the tape to a typist, who then put it in the correct screenplay form. Brian sold that first screenplay, and has written and sold many more.

Brian could have ignored his good ideas, as Hoagy Carmichael almost did. He could have spent his energy trying to learn to write as others do, or telling himself that he didn't have what it took to be a screenwriter. But instead, Brian focused on what he *could* do. That turned out to be more than enough.

PERSONAL WORK STYLE

There are as many ways to do things as there are people to do them. Do you recognize your personal style? Does your personal style fit your idea of how people should work? Or, instead of recognizing, enjoying, and benefiting from your own style, have you been trying to force yourself to adopt someone else's style— to be someone you're not? And have you then used your failure to be someone you're not as ammunition against yourself in your civil war? In my work I've discovered four distinctive personal work styles. I describe them here to give you an opportunity to think about your own personal style.

SINGLE-MINDED STYLE

People who have a single-minded style are self-starting and self-driven; they receive their motivation from an internal source. Single-minded people don't need assignments, encouragement, harassment, or deadlines to get their work done. While they're self-motivated, single-minded people *can only do one thing at a time*. Arthur, a single-minded musician, commented typically, "Whatever I'm doing at the time seems like the most important thing in the world."

People with a single-minded work style are rarely idle, so they're very productive. But they can be easily distracted, and, once disturbed, a single-minded person may have trouble finding his or her place again and continuing. Single-minded people are perfectionists. They often do what they do very well but are rarely satisfied with their performance and can always see how they could have done it better. Single-minded people are often self-critical. They consider their distractibility and their need to do one thing at a time a flaw in their makeup. Molly, a typical single-minded person, reproached herself with the notion that she could only do one thing at a time while "genius" was "the ability to hold six ideas in your head."

If you're self-driven, always working on some project; if you're self-critical, always aware of how your work could be improved; if you dismiss the compliments you receive from others; if you're most comfortable doing one thing at a time, and criticize yourself for that fact, you're most probably a single-minded person.

SCATTERGUN STYLE

Like the single-minded person, the scattergun person is self-starting. But unlike the single-minded person, the scattergun person *must do more than one thing at a time*. Scattergun people interrupt themselves; their creativity is sparked by their constantly shifting focus and attention. Louis L'Amour, the prolific writer of western fiction, had as many as three typewriters on the desk in front of him, each with a different novel in progress. He said that if he didn't move constantly back and forth, he'd lose one or another of the plots.

The hallmark of the scattergun person is that he or she is always doing more than one thing at a time. For example, a single-minded person will come home from the market and unpack and put away the groceries before doing anything else; but when scattergun people come home from the market, they may intersperse unpacking the groceries with opening the mail, making dinner, reading the newspaper, or calling a friend on the phone.

Rita Aero, a scattergun writer, explains that she chose her computer because "when I needed a break from writing, these wonderful graphics would come up and we'd play a few rounds of games, and then I'd boot my word-processing program and get back to business again."

Scattergun process is rarely acknowledged or appreciated. At a lecture I gave, a man came up to thank me. "I've always thought there was something wrong with me," he said, "because I'm compelled to read several books at a time." Scattergun people always complete what they start—if it's important—but they virtually never do anything directly from start to finish. As their priorities shift and their interest in one or another project waxes and wanes, they move fluidly back and forth.

Many people who have this work style—like the man who reads several books at a time—think there's something wrong with them because they "don't finish what they start." This misunderstanding causes many people a great deal of unnecessary distress. If you often shift your attention from one thing to another—you frequently change channels on your TV, you interrupt your homework to write a letter or phone a friend, you finish sections of several different reports before you complete one—you're a scattergun person.

ASSIGNMENT STYLE

Assignment people are just what their name implies—they need an assignment to get started. This work style may be the invention of our school system, where self-starting, creativity, or innovation, were discouraged and following directions rewarded.

Just as single-minded people need to concentrate on one thing at a time and scattergun people require many projects, people who have an assignment work style must have assignments. Their creativity is stimulated by the request for work. Matthew, a typical assignment person, is a prolific songwriter. When asked, he can write quickly and in many styles. When not asked, he can sit at the piano all day and produce very little.

Assignment people are happy and productive when they have assignments. But until they recognize their work style, they can accuse themselves of failing when, lacking an assignment, they're unproductive.

If you're blissfully happy the minute someone asks you to do something; if an assignment turns on the invisible faucet of your creativity; if you spend your energy berating yourself for not having your own ideas, you're an assignment person.

DEADLINE STYLE

Deadline people require the urgency of a deadline to get the started. They can't begin to work until they reach their particular *magic moment*. With one month, or one week, or one day—depending on the person—to go, they suddenly begin to work furiously. Don, a deadline corporate executive, complained that he's always putting the finishing touches on his report in the cab on his way to the meeting.

Deadline people *always make their deadline*, or close enough.   But until they realize that they always make their deadline, they may be miserable. People with deadline work style, like those with assignment work style, may try to trick themselves into starting early: they "ground" themselves, refusing to make plans or go out until they've begun to work; they make bets with their friends and deals with themselves; they deny themselves pleasures or promise themselves rewards; but nothing works. Until they reach their magic moment, they just can't get started.

If you regularly put off beginning the class paper, company report, or Thanksgiving dinner until *the last possible moment*; if you regularly criticize yourself for starting late; if you've ever promised yourself that this time you will get started early or tried to trick yourself into getting a "jump on things," you're a deadline person.

A SELF-APPRECIATION MOMENT

Once you understand and appreciate your style you can spend your time and energy nourishing it. Instead of criticizing yourself for being flawed you can enjoy your special style.

If you're a single-minded person, recognize that you need to focus on one thing at a time and allow for the fact that you don't take well to being disturbed. Think about constructing a work environment that satisfies these needs and in which you can be comfortable and productive. If you're a scattergun person, understand that you *need* to move from project to project, and let yourself bask in the variety of your life. If you're an assignment person, stop tormenting yourself. Start spending your energy getting assignments rather than sitting around praying for inspiration. Your assignment *is* your inspiration. If you're a deadline person, understand that you just can't get started any earlier and plan to enjoy all the extra time you have while you're waiting for your *magic moment.*

OUR PUSH-BUTTON MENTALITY

You may not have given much thought to your personal style or your personal process because our culture is more interested in results than in the processes behind them. Current technology is so fast that it seems to produce results without even going through a process—or at least without exposing its process. How many of us understand how our computer or microwave oven works? How many of us care?

Moving from the Agrarian Age to the Industrial Age was supposed to bring us prosperity and expanded leisure time. But instead of bringing us time to enjoy ourselves, our new tools

144

have just picked up the pace. Machines are faster than people, and instead of enjoying more free time, we just work faster and longer. Instead of creating the time for us to become more human, we have created a society in which we have to compete with our machines. The speed of our technology has made us impatient with ourselves and others. My friend's five-year-old daughter came home from her first day at kindergarten very disappointed. "The teachers don't sing and dance and disappear the way they do on 'Sesame Street,'" she complained.

Machines are faster, more consistent, and more predictable than human beings. But we are not machines, we are people, and there's no point in our trying to become like machines. Now that we have machines to do the things that they do so well, we have an opportunity to allow ourselves to explore the limits of being truly human, to revel in what we can do that machines cannot do: feel, create, invent, forgive, love.

READY OR NOT, I WILL CHANGE

Our culture likes speed—the faster something can be done, the better. Information that used to come by mail now comes by fax or modem. The mail came only once or twice a day, but the fax and the modem are ever present. There used to be time for us to think about and plan our responses, but today we barely have time to think about—much less process, prepare, develop, or formulate—what we want to say, before we're expected to respond. Consequently, we've forgotten that some things, like human change, still take time. Some changes need to be incubated or developed, to mature and ripen before they can occur.

Many of us believe that "good" or "normal" people can force themselves into making whatever changes they want or need to make. Consequently, the pressure to try to change— even when you can't—is very strong. In response to this pressure you may be willing to try any trick, hoping that it will help you quickly become whoever it is your conscious mind thinks you have to be. But these "tricks" that are supposed to help you change rarely work, since they disregard the resistance of your unconscious mind—which will not be tricked and will work against the change until you're ready to tolerate its consequences. When these methods—some of which seemed to work for others—fail, you feel much worse than you did before. You may blame yourself for the failure and suffer lowered self-esteem. And when you feel bad about yourself, you are less likely to be able to act in your own best interests.

Our society's instant-soup and hurry-up messages are pervasive and make it very difficult for you to trust that when you *can* change, you *will*. Many try to jump-start the change they want to make, hoping that if they can just get started, however artificially, they can somehow find a way to maintain their momentum.

The following are some of the methods I've observed people using when they're trying to manufacture a change they couldn't make naturally and easily. You may recognize some of these methods as ones that you've tried. In your zeal to make the change, you may not realize that the method you're using isn't actually working. As you read this section, ask yourself if you've tried any of these methods and if they've helped you make a lasting change.

KNOWING BETTER

How often have you, or someone you know, said "How could I have done that? I know better." As I pointed out in chapter 5, information, awareness, and understanding—the province of the conscious mind—are highly valued in this society. We believe that if we can only *know why* we do something, we will be able to change it.

In therapy, knowledge is called *insight*. Many people have been disappointed when, having gained insight in therapy, they still couldn't make the change they wanted to make. George Gershwin told his friend Oscar Levant that, while he hadn't solved the problem for which he entered analysis, at least he now knew why he had it.

One of the reasons some people spend years in therapy with seemingly little result is that *knowing better* is not enough to make you able to change. You must be able to endure the consequences the change will bring before you can risk making it. Knowledge alone won't create that ability. Knowing better may satisfy the curiosity of the conscious mind, but it rarely helps people change their behavior.

Marla came into therapy armed with the books she'd read and her own diagnosis. "I'm co-dependent," she announced. She described a childhood in which her alcoholic father was alternately charming and terrifying. As an adult, Marla was attracted to men who were charming at the beginning of the relationship, but soon became cruel. Having seen their cruel side, however, Marla couldn't break off the relationship. "Why do I keep doing this?" she asked. "When I, of all people, should know better!"

Her father's violence forced Marla to adopt a *victim* cover. She had no defense against him and didn't dare "stand up" to him. Her *victim* cover kept her docile and, as much as possible, out of harm's way. At the same time her unconscious mind protected her by hiding her *power* and *assertiveness*—qualities that would have endangered her—safely under cover.

As a child, Marla connected *power* and *assertiveness* with her father's cruelty. As an adult, she'd been proud of her own *kindness* and *passivity* and critical of people who were *pushy* or *just out for themselves*. Unfortunately, it was precisely these qualities that Marla needed to stand up to and protect herself from the abusive men in her present life.

In therapy, Marla did gain knowledge. She recognized that power and assertiveness aren't necessarily cruel. She learned that it was the recovery of her own power and not finding "a good man" that would help her achieve the relationship she wanted. Simply knowing why she got involved with abusive men, understanding that she was duplicating a pattern from her past, didn't help Marla break the pattern. But the knowledge that Marla gained in therapy helped her shift her attention from her camouflage problem, that of trying to find the right man, to her real problem, which was appreciating and reclaiming her own personal power.

Knowing why you do something pleases your conscious mind, and if used correctly, such knowledge can be an important part—but not the whole—of your strategy for change. Knowledge that helps you shift your attention off a camouflage problem, forgive yourself for not changing, or unhook from a civil war, can enhance your life. But if you're expecting knowledge alone to make you able to change, you'll probably be disappointed.

BUCKLE DOWN

When knowledge fails, you may try discipline, hoping that willpower, self-control, self-denial, or persistence will help you become the person you want to be. Self-discipline can work for a while. But if you can't face the consequences of the change you want to make, even the most dedicated self-discipline will provide only a short-term solution, and will ultimately fail.

"White-knuckling it," or using willpower to break a habit, is a highly regarded, if mostly inefficient, method of making changes in our culture. This method also overestimates the power of the conscious mind, and underestimates the power of the unconscious. The unconscious can wipe away the most dedicated attempts at willpower with a whim, an impulse, or remembering to forget. One evening I watched as a friend of mine, who had quit smoking, lit a cigarette. When I said that I thought he'd quit, he looked with astonishment at his hand and said, "I have stopped, I didn't realize that I'd picked it up." As long as you aren't ready to endure the consequences of the change you want to make, neither willpower nor self-discipline will have the desired effect.

Rhea came to see me to put an end to a lifelong weight problem. At 32 she called herself "the diet queen." She'd done them all. While she was on a diet Rhea was remarkably disciplined and nothing could make her "cheat." But whenever a diet started to work and she began to lose weight, Rhea felt "little, helpless, and scared" and immediately began to put the pounds back on. Her life had been a seesaw of losing and gaining weight, but no matter how self-disciplined she was, she couldn't keep it off. As long as Rhea needed her extra pounds to feel safe, all of her discipline couldn't help her keep the weight off.

I suggested to Rhea that feeling safe was a very good reason for staying big and asked her what might be making her feel unsafe. After thinking about it, Rhea wondered if it might have something to do with the fact that her brother had molested her when they were children. Until that moment, Rhea's conscious mind hadn't made the connection between her inability to lose weight and the abuse she suffered as a child. Rhea was only 8 years old when her 13-year-old brother began to molest her. As she talked about the terrible experience, she recalled that at the time she'd thought, "If only I were bigger, I could stop him."

As an adult, whenever she got "small," the fear of those early years threatened to erupt and only subsided when she was once again "big." To Rhea, her safety depended on her size, and as long as being "safe" also meant being big she couldn't lose weight.

Rhea remembered *what* happened to her when she was a child, but she didn't remember how she'd *felt* when it happened. When she became physically small, however, the feelings of terror and helplessness, which had been unbearable for her when she was a child, reappeared.

I explained to Rhea that if she was ready to endure the pain of her past, her unconscious would let her feel the feelings it had been helping her deny. I asked her to close her eyes,

149

imagine that she was already small, and by paying attention to her body, notice any physical sensation she experienced as she imagined this. Rhea shuddered. She felt "shaky in her arms and chest," she said. I then asked Rhea to concentrate on the places that had the "shaky" feeling and ask her unconscious if it could give her the information—which it had stored in her body—in a way that her conscious mind could better understand. Rhea began to cry. "I can see him climbing on top of me," she said. "I'm crying and telling him to stop, but he looks so mean and so angry. I'm very scared."

The 32-year-old woman became a frightened 8-year-old child. Rhea cried and cried; she was beginning to reclaim a part of herself that she'd long had to deny—a hurt and terrified little girl. It felt awful, but it had been her inability to bear these terrible feelings that had stopped Rhea from losing weight.

It took time for Rhea to express all of the terrible feelings she'd kept buried for so many years. It took time for her to realize that she could bear the feelings and to learn how to comfort herself when they occurred. As she was more and more able to comfort herself, Rhea was less and less frightened by the feelings that being small triggered. As her fear of her feelings diminished, Rhea's self-discipline finally started to pay off, and she began slowly but surely to lose the weight that had been a protection she no longer needed.

Solutions that depend on self-discipline alone are too hard to keep up because they don't address the very good reason you have for not changing. If you're not ready to face the larger danger, your unconscious will see to it that your attempts fail. When you fail you may feel bad about yourself and resort to another popular strategy—criticism.

BAD ME

You may believe, as many people do, that you can criticize or scold yourself into changing. You really could change, you think, but you're too lazy or stubborn to do so on your own. You disapprove of yourself and tell yourself and others just how bad you are. Basically you treat yourself like a naughty child who will only respond to punishment. But instead of helping you change, calling yourself names like *lazy, stubborn, hung-up, weak, procrastinating,* or *self-destructive* will just make you feel worse.

It might seem obvious, but when people who believe that criticism will make them change come to see me, I tell them that the distress of not being able to do what they want to do is punishment enough. They don't deserve to pile the agony of self-recrimination onto the agony they're already experiencing, and, I add, it won't work anyway.

When you're making a change that requires you to confront a personal danger, encouragement and sympathy can really help, and criticism can really hurt. Unfortunately, people who believe in criticism generally surround themselves with like-minded friends who join in the commentary. Lee came into therapy to get her boyfriend, John, to move out of their apartment. "I'm tired of taking care of him," she said, "but I've never lived alone and I'm afraid to try it." Lee's *dependent* cover persuaded her that she couldn't live alone, and her fear of living alone convinced her that she was inadequate.

In therapy Lee worked on reclaiming the *self-reliant* under cover she'd learned to deny in childhood. When she was in touch with her emerging self-reliance, she felt strong and told John to leave. Then she'd forget that she could take care of herself, experience herself as *dependent,* have an anxiety attack, and ask John to come back.

Swinging back and forth between wanting to be rid of John and her fear of being alone, Lee kept changing her mind. When she gave in, Lee criticized herself mercilessly, and her friends agreed with her brutal self-assessment. Lee's friends were so critical of what they called her "wimp" behavior that she was afraid to tell them when she let John move back in. She tried to keep her reunions with John a secret, but when the need to talk about what was happening to her became too great, she'd break down and confide in her friends, who would then accuse her of being "stupid" and "cowardly." All of this scolding, however well intentioned, undermined rather than encouraged her attempts to reclaim her self-reliance. Every criticism verified her *inadequate* and *dependent* covers, making her feel worse about herself and more afraid to risk being alone.

Criticism lowers self-esteem and increases anxiety. When you're anxious and dislike yourself, you're less able to do even the easy things—much less take the risks that the difficult changes almost always require. Criticism may temporarily alter behavior, but as long as your unconscious mind recognizes a danger your conscious mind cannot see, it will stop you from changing. No amount of criticism will change that.

Knowing better, discipline, and criticism are some of the most popular methods to make yourself change, but they aren't the only ones.

KEEPING YOUR EYE ON THE BALL

In sports we're instructed to keep our eye on the ball. Many people try this approach to create change in their lives. They narrow their field of vision and focus all of their attention on the change. But success can require a shift of attention away from the change you want to make—taking your eye off the ball. This can be true even in sports.

During a tennis lesson my forehand stopped working. I tried everything I "knew" about how to hit a forehand, but I couldn't correct it. I was very frustrated. Finally, my instructor suggested that I extend my follow-through so that when I finished the stroke, my racquet would be in my opposite hand. I really had to concentrate to do this. I stopped thinking about correcting my forehand and focused all my attention on making the racquet come out in my left hand. My forehand corrected itself.

When you focus too closely on the problem, you limit your options. When you use only what your conscious mind "knows," you may only see the solutions you've already tried and be stuck reusing solutions that have already failed. New solutions may be necessary and your unconscious may be sending them to you, but when you're committed to the old solutions you may not notice the new ones. When you find yourself going around and around in the same old circles, a shift of attention can allow you to receive information from your unconscious mind.

Tina had hated her job in advertising for a long time, but she couldn't see any way out of it. The only solution her conscious mind could think of was to keep telling herself that it wasn't that bad and she could do it. But this pep talk didn't work, and finally her unconscious mind took the decision out of her hands.

One day Tina started to cry and couldn't make herself stop. She was forced to take a leave of absence, and while she was recuperating, getting ready to resume the life she hated, Tina had a "silly idea." She enrolled in a flower-arranging class. It was something she'd always thought of doing, but had never had the time to do.

She found that she loved arranging flowers and had a real talent for it. She got more involved in her "hobby" and began to dread going back to "work," when a friend asked Tina to arrange flowers for a party she was having. Without her conscious mind recognizing it, Tina was beginning a new career. The only solution her conscious mind had been able to offer was more of the same, but once Tina could stop and listen to herself, her unconscious was able to point the way to a new solution.

Every year I fertilize the same patch of ground and plant vegetables. One year, after preparing the soil, I ran out of steam and couldn't do any planting. In the spring, to my amazement, I had a beautiful bed of snapdragons. Just as I didn't know that snapdragon seeds lay dormant below the surface, waiting for the space and nourishment to burst into beautiful flower, so you may be unaware of the skills, talents, interests, abilities, and pleasures that wait patiently within you, looking for an opportunity to enrich your life.

The stubborn belief that what you "know" is all that you are will cause you to shortchange yourself. When you *unfocus*, take your eye off the ball, you allow your unconscious mind to offer outrageous options. Then wonderful alternatives and solutions become possible.

THE ONE-SIZE-FITS-ALL SOLUTION

Many people believe that there's a *one-size-fits-all* solution to problems. If a solution worked for someone else, then it should work for us, too, we reason. Following this logic, businesses use celebrity endorsements to demonstrate that this or that product worked for someone we are likely to admire. Not only celebrities and those we want to emulate, but anyone who seems to have done what we want to do, can become a model for our behavior.

Jane came into therapy to find out why she allowed the men in her life to neglect her. She'd been trying to solve this problem for years. She said she'd even tried a solution she learned from a casual acquaintance. At a party she met Helen and Dan, who, in their mid-30s, were deliriously happy newlyweds. Helen confided to Jane that she'd always dated uncaring men until one day she'd just had enough and promised herself that no man was ever going to mistreat her again, even if it meant that she'd be alone forever. To her surprise she soon met and married Dan, who was wonderful to her.

Jane wanted what Helen had, and decided to adopt Helen's technique. Jane promised herself that she'd no longer let a man get away with neglecting her. She tried, but she couldn't do it. When her boyfriend ignored her, she couldn't think of anything to do about it.

Jane learned her *invisible* cover by modeling her mother, a sad and neglected woman who dutifully cared for her husband

and never complained. Jane's father was an unresponsive man who made a living for his family but was emotionally unavailable to his wife and child. Jane not only copied her mother's *invisible* cover, but, recognizing her mother's unhappiness, came to feel responsible for her.

Staying neglected was one of the ways Jane protected her mother. To Jane, standing up for herself meant hurting her mother's feelings. It would be like saying to her mother, "I did it, why couldn't you?"

In therapy Jane realized that before she could be demanding in a relationship with a man, she had to give up being responsible for her mother. In other words, she had to neglect her mother. Realizing this, she shifted her attention from trying to get her boyfriend to change to separating from her mother.

Jane still called her mother, but not nearly as often as before, and when they talked, Jane no longer encouraged her mother to complain about her father. She attended family gatherings, but took on less responsibility; she didn't offer to do more than her share of the work, even when that meant that her mother was overburdened. As she changed her behavior, Jane began to see how her mother participated in her own neglect and how she, Jane, had been chosen by the family to take care of Mom in her father's emotional absence.

When Jane constructed her family pie she saw clearly that the qualities of *self-containment* and *indifference* belonged to her father and that she perceived these as masculine qualities. *Responsibility* and *invisibility*, on the other hand, were assigned to Jane and her mother as feminine qualities. When Jane started to change, she unbalanced the whole family and they joined forces to try to stop her. Her father broke a lifetime unwritten code by calling Jane to see if she was all right and to tell her that her mother's feelings were hurt by Jane's apparent neglect. After her father, Jane's aunt called to scold Jane for neglecting her mother. Even Jane's cousin, prompted by her mother, Jane's aunt, called to try to get Jane back in line. I had warned Jane that when she was able to change, there would probably be a reaction from her family. The power of the reaction was proof to Jane that she was indeed changing.

As she changed her relationship with the members of her family, Jane noticed that, without really trying, she'd begun to behave differently in her relationship with her boyfriend. Suddenly she was no longer so afraid of hurting his feelings or losing him. Whereas before she'd been unable to think of any appropriate response to his neglect, now she was full of ideas. She teased him for his self-centeredness, and even began to neglect him. The balance of this relationship is changing and the conclusion is not yet clear. But what is clear is that Jane has renounced her *invisible* cover, and for her, nothing will be exactly the same as it has been.

There are no *one-size-fits-all* solutions to problems. It's tempting to hope that the answer is out there and that someone else—a friend, a parent, a member of the clergy, or a therapist— can tell you what it is; but the answer is in you. While some of those people can provide support, encouragement, advice, information, or help, no one else's answer is necessarily the right answer, because no one else's answer is necessarily your answer. If someone else's answer hasn't worked for you, don't worry—it doesn't mean there's something wrong with you, it just means there's something wrong with the answer.

GIVE YOURSELF A BREAK

In my office I often find myself sitting across from unhappy people who have courageously presented themselves for the browbeating, tongue-lashing, or humiliation they expect me to deliver. "I'm bad (or wrong or sick)," they say, "don't give me an inch, make me do right!" But over and over again I've seen that it's only when they finally let themselves *off* the hook—give up trying to be right, correct, or normal—and begin to appreciate, care for, and love themselves *just as they are*, that the seemingly impossible changes finally take place.

- *Knowing* why you have a hated habit you still can't break fosters self-contempt.
- *Disciplining* yourself and finding that you cheat anyway can be very discouraging.
- *Criticizing* yourself will undermine, rather than motivate, you.
- *Focusing* too closely on the problem can keep you from seeing the solution.
- *Using* someone else's *one-size-fits-all* solution to problems can delay your search for your own solution.

The sooner you shift your attention from regret and criticism to discovery and appreciation, the sooner you can tailor your life to reflect who you are. The more your life reflects who you really are, the happier and more comfortable you'll be.

In this chapter I've talked about the pressure on each of us to be "good," "correct," or "normal," and the methods many of us use in our attempts to live up to these cultural ideas of who we have to be. In the next chapter, I'll show you what it means to be ready to make the difficult changes and what you can expect to happen when you are indeed ready to make them.

Readiness— There's No Getting Around It

I f you've attempted to make the stubborn changes, or if you've tried some or all of the methods of forcing change that I talked about in the last chapter, and they haven't worked, this may be because some changes cannot be made no matter

- how much you want to make them,
- how hard you try to make them, or
- what tricks you use to force yourself to make them, until you are *ready* to make them.

You may want to be ready. You may think you should be ready. You may believe that you are ready. Other people may insist that you're ready. But what you or others want, think, or believe won't make you ready. *You will be ready to change only when—no matter what happens—you can survive the dangers change will bring.*

Sometimes, when I tell people that they are just not yet ready to change, they think that I'm encouraging them to accept their pain and do nothing about it. *But I'm not saying "Don't want," "Don't try," or "Don't do."* By all means go ahead and do everything you can do. But if you *have* tried, and repeatedly failed, to make this change, then I repeat: It may be because you're just not ready to make this change at this time. Readiness cannot be counterfeited, imitated, or manufactured. You can't pretend to be ready.

CONSCIOUS CONTROL VS. UNCONSCIOUS CONTROL

The idea that unaided wanting and trying can create change is seductive because it puts the power to change in the control of your conscious mind, whose activities you "know." But it is your unconscious mind that decides when you're ready to change, and to paraphrase an old TV commercial, "You can't fool your unconscious."

You're an essentially self-protective person. You will not make changes that put you in too much danger. That you don't recognize the danger doesn't mean it isn't there. Your unconscious sees it and will shield you until the very moment that you can endure and survive it. The moment you are *ready*, you will change—sometimes quite suddenly.

Just as your conscious mind can be blind to the danger that keeps you from changing, it may also miss the moment you become ready to change. Then your unconscious, which has so successfully obstructed the change, will *initiate* it. Your unconscious will urge you to do what your conscious mind may not realize you've become ready to do. When you're ready to change, you *will* change—the "easy way" or the "hard way."

THE EASY WAY

Changes made the easy way are spontaneous and effortless. They are achieved without struggle or distress, and sometimes without awareness. Suddenly, without even realizing it, you're different.

You were poised at the growing edge, wanting to do something you'd never done before, or you were standing at the tip of the diving board, wanting to do something that had awful consequences the last time you did it. You'd been trying to push yourself into change, but you couldn't do it. Then your unconscious looked out at the drop below and said, "You may not like all of the consequences of the change you want to make, but you can tolerate even the worst that may happen." And the next thing you knew, you were standing in midair, having quite casually and naturally stepped out into what looked like a void. Suddenly, without fanfare or bells and whistles, you changed.

THE MOMENT OF CHANGE. A day ago you couldn't do it, but today you're asking your boss for a raise, filling out an application for graduate school, or saying, "Yes, I'll marry you." When the change you couldn't make just yesterday isn't so difficult anymore, you've changed the easy way.

Think back upon the difficult changes you've made in your life, the ones you struggled with and then finally accomplished: the times, when after months or years of effort, debate, therapy, encouragement, and failed attempts, you were finally able to quit your job, stand up for yourself, sign up for piano lessons, lose weight, stop drinking, arrive on time, or have an orgasm.

Do you remember the moment you changed—the moment you went from being someone who couldn't to someone who could? Or is the memory of that moment a little hazy? Do you recall *how* you did it? You may be able to sharply remember the before and after—the struggle and the success—but the actual moment of change may be unclear, clouded. You may know what you did to cause the change, but not what actually changed—why you were finally able to do what had been impossible before.

William James, the 19th-century psychologist and philosopher, illustrated this point by using a dilemma faced by people who live in cold climates. In the morning, he said, you

161

wake in a warm bed knowing you'll have to leave it for a cold room and an icy floor. You lie there, and you don't want to get up. You can't make yourself get up. Then suddenly you *are* up. Something has changed. One moment you couldn't, and the next moment you could. You've passed through the moment of change. You may remember lying in a warm bed, wishing you'd never have to leave it. You may remember the feel of the icy floor on your warm toes. But the exact moment of change, when you went from one to the other, is very often fuzzy and difficult to recall.

You know how much you wanted to change, and you know what you did to try to cause it, because wanting and trying are functions of the conscious mind and you're aware of its activities. You don't know when you actually changed because readiness is monitored by your unconscious mind, which functions out of your awareness. This paradox makes it possible for you do something and not know why.

I have seen this phenomenon repeated over and over. For weeks, months, and sometimes years, people will struggle. "I can't stand this pain," they'll say. "I want to be different. I have to change." Then one day, they simply turn a corner—they stop hurting and start to feel good. They are different. They have changed.

Jordan came to see me to find out why she couldn't fall in love. A lovely, intelligent woman who had a career as a legal secretary, she was often pursued by the lawyers and interns at her office, but she just didn't like any of them. For years she'd thought this was just because she was "picky," but at 37, she was beginning to wonder if there wasn't something else going on.

Jordan described her relationship with her family as "very close." When she moved out of her parents' home at age 26 she'd rented an apartment a block away. She loved the neighborhood, she said, and liked being near her family. During her therapy Jordan realized that her "very close" relationship with her family was actually blocking her ability to establish a close relationship with a man. When I asked Jordan if she'd ever considered moving away from the family neighborhood, she said that she'd often thought about buying a condo, which she could well afford, but had never been able to start the process.

I suggested that Jordan daydream about her new condo—where it might be, what it might look like, how it might feel to really be on her own. Jordan was astonished to discover that whenever she thought about finding "a home of her own," she got anxious. She worried that the dry cleaner wouldn't know her, or that the grocery store would be unfamiliar, or that she'd have to get acquainted with a whole new set of neighbors.

In therapy Jordan continued to explore ways that she could begin the separation process from her family. She drew a family pie and discovered her role as the "family pet," someone her parents could "pamper and spoil." Whenever the question of moving away came up, Jordan said that it was just too scary for her to think about.

One day Jordan came to her session grinning broadly. "I did it," she said. "I bought a condo. I don't know exactly what happened. I saw this sign on a building in the neighborhood I used to daydream about and for some reason it just didn't seem scary to go ahead and do it, so I did." Moving away from her family was the beginning of the separation Jordan badly needed to accomplish before she could commit herself to a relationship. She was ready to begin this process, and so she found her condo the easy way.

Even when she was unable to find her condo, Jordan knew what she wanted to do, but knowing isn't necessary. When you're ready to change, you will make the right change even when you don't "know" what it is.

You may, for example, be ready to accept and integrate a previously denied under cover quality, but your conscious mind doesn't "know" it. Your conscious mind may still think you need to pretend that you are never *silly*, or *stubborn*, or *unconventional*. It may still think of this quality as "bad." At these times your unconscious mind may help you un-cover this quality by causing you to act in this bad way.

163

Paul came into therapy to find out why he always fell in love with women who took advantage of him. Paul had a *good boy* cover, which he'd adopted as the oldest child of a chronically ill mother, and which he lived up to in therapy. He never missed a session, he always arrived early, he followed instructions, did his homework, and answered any question he was asked.

When we talked about his cover and how it operated in his life, I told Paul that he probably had a *bad boy* under cover and that I'd certainly like to see it in action. Paul was intrigued, even a bit excited at the prospect, but said that he just couldn't be bad. After six months in therapy, one day he forgot to bring his checkbook. The following week he brought the checkbook, but was horrified to discover that he was out of checks. Paul was very concerned. This was, to say the least, very unlike him.

I asked Paul how he felt when he realized that he wasn't going to be able to pay me. He said that even though he knew it was "crazy," he thought that I wouldn't see him, and even that I might "throw him out."

Despite himself, Paul was revealing what he considered his worst side to me. He was being his *bad* self—the one who didn't put my needs first; he was risking abandonment. All of his life Paul had been afraid that if he angered or disappointed a woman he cared for, she'd leave him. It was that fear that had forced him to accept bad treatment while continuing to act like the *good boy*. After this experience Paul noticed that he was less willing to "roll over." He even got angry at, and once in a while said no to, his current girlfriend, behaviors that were previously unthinkable.

WHO DID THAT? When you make a change the easy way, the transition can be so smooth that you don't "know" you've changed. You may not realize that you're acting differently. The new behavior is so natural that it doesn't feel uncomfortable or awkward. It may take the comments of other people, or the recognition that something that had eluded you is now in your grasp, before your conscious mind realizes that you've changed.

As long as Nadine could remember she'd wanted to go to Europe. It was her favorite daydream. She talked about it all through high school and college but she had a *timid* cover and never considered going alone. After college she got a job that allowed her a two-week vacation. Nadine thought this was a good time to go to Europe, but couldn't find anyone to go with her.

Consciously, Nadine continued to think of herself as *timid*, someone who was afraid to travel alone. She bought airline tickets, made hotel reservations, and began to read books on the countries she planned to visit, oblivious to the unusual nature of her behavior.

When the trip was a week away, Nadine's conscious mind suddenly woke up. "Who bought these tickets?" it asked. "Who made these plans? It couldn't have been me, I'm too afraid to go to Europe alone!" But by then it was too late to change her plans, so she went and had a wonderful time.

Changes made the easy way can represent a major departure from the way you're accustomed to doing things and the way you're accustomed to thinking about yourself. The new behavior can seem so foreign that, although it's clearly you who are saying and doing these things, it feels as though it's someone else saying and doing them. You may feel like an observer watching someone—you—as you act in this new and startling way.

Francine wanted to buy a house. She was "tired of renting and tired of living in someone else's house" she said. She wanted "a place of her own with a backyard"; she wanted to make her own statement. She could easily afford to buy a house but somehow she couldn't make herself do it. "It seemed," she said, "like too much to ask for."

In therapy Francine discovered her *assertive* under cover and was learning to separate what she truly wanted from what she thought should satisfy her. She'd begun to honor her needs even when it sometimes meant overlooking the needs of others.

Once in a while she found herself uncharacteristically saying no, refusing to allow friends to impose on her. This was very difficult for Francine, because she was discovering that it could be dangerous to put her needs first. Her attempts to un-cover were so compelling and required so much of her attention that she stopped thinking about buying a house. But her unconscious hadn't stopped paying attention. When it decided that she could bear the consequences of really putting her needs first, it acted.

One day, quite spontaneously, Francine called a realtor and made plans to go out and look at houses. Before meeting the realtor, she assured herself that she was just going to look, not to buy. "It never occurred to me that I was actually going to buy a house," she said. "I thought that I was just doing the ground-work for the time when I became ready. I was astonished when I heard myself agreeing to put in a bid. It wasn't me talking."

This feeling that it's "not you" engaging in the behavior is one of the hallmarks of changing the easy way. You're so *ready* that you slip naturally into the change before your conscious mind has a chance to realize it.

CONVENIENT MISTAKES. As I illustrated in chapters 5 and 6, your unconscious uses many tricks to keep you from changing before you're ready. It can use these same tricks to nudge you into change when you're ready but don't realize it.

One of the unconscious mind's favorite tricks is helping you make "convenient mistakes." This is occurring when you do something you didn't intend to do—you make a mistake—and you later realize that this *mistake* is the very change you were trying to make. When you're changing the easy way, like Ken in the following example, you can even enjoy watching yourself "mess up."

Ken came into therapy to learn how to stand up for himself. His tall good looks belied his *pushover* cover. A conscientious employee who was very good at his job, Ken accepted bad treatment from his dictatorial boss and was afraid to stand up for himself or quit. At least once a week, when his boss did something to embarrass, insult, or take advantage of him, Ken's determination to "get the hell out of there" was rekindled. But when he thought seriously about quitting his job, his *pushover* cover popped up; he worried about appearing *pushy* and backed down.

In therapy Ken drew his family pie and realized that he probably had an *assertive* under cover. The qualities of stubbornness and overbearingness showed up in the pie pieces of several of his family members, and Ken realized that he'd adopted his *pushover* cover to provide his family with someone they could push around.

With his new knowledge, Ken assiduously tried to reclaim his *assertive* under cover. He daydreamed about telling his boss off; he practiced his quitting speech. But no matter how he tried to make himself act differently, he couldn't do it. In the heat of the moment he forgot everything he'd rehearsed and acted in the *responsible* and *pushover* way he always had.

One Friday afternoon his boss, imposing once again, asked Ken to take a proposal home and study it over the weekend. Ken was angry, but he said he'd do it. When he got home he was surprised to discover that he'd forgotten to take the proposal with him. Ken was delighted to see that despite himself, he was refusing to be pushed around.

Your unconscious mind, by helping you make a convenient mistake, can accomplish the easy way what your conscious mind has wanted and tried, but failed, to do.

IT CAN'T BE THAT EASY. You may not trust a change so easily made. You may not believe that a change you struggled with and were unable to make could be made the easy way. Significant changes, like the contradiction of a cover story, can be difficult to accept. When you've believed for most of your life that you're a particular kind of person and then you suddenly find that you're someone else—even when the new you is just who you always hoped you'd be—the change can be hard to believe. It can be hard to trust that it isn't some sneaky fairy godmother's trick that is destined to fade on the stroke of midnight. Even seeing yourself act in the new way may not be enough to convince your conscious mind that you've really changed.

It may take time to get used to being the new you. Indeed, even after you've acknowledged your new identity, you may occasionally forget that you changed. When Carter invited his girlfriend, Rose, to accompany him to a friend's wedding, he warned her that he didn't like big parties and didn't expect to have a good time.

Contrary to what he'd said, Carter appeared to have a wonderful time, and as they drove home he talked glowingly about the party. Rose was baffled. "But I thought you didn't like big parties," she said. "Oh," he replied, "that was the old me. I forgot that I'd changed!"

This is a more common occurrence than you might think. It can be difficult for the conscious mind to trust that you have changed. Since your conscious mind didn't participate in, or even observe, the change as it happened, to your conscious mind the change didn't actually happen. It may explain away your new behavior as some kind of fluke, which can't possibly last.

If you find yourself second-guessing a change you've made the easy way, don't worry. Your conscious mind doesn't have to believe in the change for it to last. If you can tolerate the consequences of the change, despite what your conscious mind believes, even changes that happen in a heartbeat will last.

It is *readiness and not intention* that makes change possible. When readiness is present, even some of the most difficult changes can be made the easy way. But there are changes that will hurt no matter how ready you are to make them. They are the changes that must be made the "hard way."

THE HARD WAY

Changes made the hard way are just what they sound like. Instead of sliding gently into change, you feel like you're being pushed and pulled against your will. When you're changing the hard way you can feel like the rope in a game of tug-of-war. Your unconscious—pulling one way—says you're *ready* and initiates the change, but your conscious—pulling the other way— opposes the change and tries to stop it.

The change you need to make and are ready to make—the change you're about to make—may not be a change your conscious mind *wants* you to make. The intensity of your conscious mind's objection to the change determines if changing the hard way will be simply unpleasant or excruciating.

When your conscious mind challenges the change you're about to make, your unconscious mind must do something to override its veto. Your unconscious mind must find a way to help you change despite the disapproval of your conscious mind. The unconscious often solves this problem by generating a tremendous wind up there at the growing edge or the tip of the diving board. When the wind hits you, you lose your balance. You begin to sway on the precipice and then spiral downward. You're being launched into change, but to most of us it just feels like falling.

When you're changing the hard way, although a part of you—your unconscious mind—is directing your actions, it can feel as though someone else is pulling your strings. If you don't see the hand of your unconscious in what's happening to you, you may feel out of control and be frightened.

Renouncing a cover quality on which your self-esteem has depended and re-covering the under cover quality you believe will expose you as "bad" is a change that is often made the hard way.

Janice came to see me because she was afraid that there was something wrong with her. In her life she'd always been

169

able to make herself do whatever she wanted to do whenever she wanted to do it. But now, no matter how she tried to force herself, she couldn't make herself do a simple thing. For three weeks Janice had planned to spend her one day off rising early to do chores. She planned to go to the bank and the cleaners, then return home and work in the garden. But when Sunday came she couldn't budge. "I spent the whole day in bed watching TV," she said. "It was awful. I must be losing my mind."

Janice was a high-powered attorney who was very proud of her energy, accomplishments, and *go-getter* cover. She'd been working a grueling six-day work week for a year. Consciously, she strongly disapproved of *goofing off* and anyone who did it. But she was exhausted and needed her under cover ability to *rest* and *relax* to keep her from burning out.

Her unconscious took the matter out of her conscious hands by disabling her and forcing her to rest. Instead of relaxing and enjoying this badly needed break, Janice's conscious mind judged it as *goofing off*, making it impossible for her to appreciate the self-protective gift her unconscious mind had given her.

When you demonstrate an under cover quality you've previously had to deny, your conscious mind, like Janice's, may disapprove. Unable to recognize the value of this new ability, it may worry that you won't be able to recapture the cover ability. But be assured, you haven't lost your cover—Janice could still *get up and go*—you've just gained access to a part of yourself you didn't know you had, and, again like Janice, probably badly need.

REFEELING. Another change that often has to be made the hard way is the recapturing of an emotion you previously had to deny. In our rational and conscious society, being "emotional" is considered a weakness and discouraged. There's pressure from movies, songs, TV, novels, commercials, and peers to be "cool."

A result of this pervasive emotion bashing is that many people are embarrassed by their emotions. They try not to feel, and when they can't stop themselves from feeling, they then discount what they feel. "Forgive me," they say, "I'm just being emotional," implying that their emotions are not real or credible. "It's just my emotions talking," they say. "They don't count." But the opposite is true—your emotions are what is most authentic about you. They are the best gauge of what's going on inside of you, the legitimate measure of your pain and your pleasure. When you are separated from your emotions, you are separated from yourself.

Still, the taboo against feeling is very powerful and has forced many of us to deny what we feel—to deny ourselves. Your family may have their own prohibition against feelings. If you were told by your family to keep your problems to yourself, or not to wash your dirty linen in public, the change you may have to make the hard way may be simply to *feel*.

You may be ready to tolerate the reexperiencing of a painful feeling you buried many years ago; but your conscious mind doesn't know about the buried pain, so how can it recognize your readiness to reexperience it?

At 32, Sarah wanted be in a committed relationship. She dated often, but whenever she was with a man she liked, Sarah acted in a way she didn't recognize. "It's not me who's saying and doing all those stupid things," she said. "It's a stranger." Sarah realized that something other than her conscious mind was affecting her behavior, but she didn't know what, and she didn't like it.

When Sarah was 12 years old her father, whom she loved very much, died suddenly. He went to work one day as usual and just didn't come home. In a mistaken attempt to protect her, Sarah's mother kept her from the funeral and discouraged her expressions of grief. Sarah was never really sure that her father had died. Maybe, she thought, he went away because he didn't want to be with her.

There was no one to help Sarah through this terrible time. The thought that her father might have run away from her, and her unexpressed grief, were too awful to bear. Her unconscious protected her by burying these thoughts and feelings deep inside her, out of the sight of her conscious mind. Now, although she didn't realize it, Sarah was afraid to fall in love, afraid that if she once again lost a loved one, the unbearable feelings she'd successfully hidden would be triggered. To keep her from establishing the kind of relationship that would endanger her, Sarah's unconscious helped her act like a "stranger" with men she liked.

When she came to see me, Sarah was ready to reexperience the pain of her past. When I explained the connection between her grief over her father's death and her strange behavior with men, she received a flood of memories and feelings she thought she'd forgotten. She remembered her father, how much she'd loved him, and how much she'd missed him. She moved deeper and deeper into the lost pain of her past, finally reliving her terrible feelings of loss and the awful suspicion that her father hadn't died, but just left her. Sarah was surprised at the power and presence of these memories and feelings. They seemed to be waiting there just below the surface. "It's as though it's happening now," she said, "instead of twenty years ago."

After this experience, without realizing it, Sarah was less afraid of falling in love. The worst that could happen to her was that she'd lose a loved one, and she now knew that, although it would certainly hurt her, she could survive such a loss. Sarah was surprised to notice that now when she was with a man she liked, she was more often *herself* and no longer a *stranger*.

When the change you have to make requires you to feel an emotion you've always condemned, your conscious mind may rise up to oppose its expression. The objection from your conscious mind may take the form of an internal dialogue in which you accuse yourself of being bad, weak, childish, foolish, or stupid. You might feel shame, disgust, or self-contempt. You may think that you're crazy or that you'll never be yourself again—that person who doesn't cry, laugh, or tremble. But if your unconscious mind has determined that you're ready to feel this emotion and integrate this aspect of yourself, you will feel it. The assault from your conscious mind won't stop you from changing, but it may affect the nature of the change you make; this kind of change will have to be accomplished the hard way.

For 30 years Arlene prided herself on an *I don't show my feelings* cover, hiding her emotions safely and deeply under cover. Her unconscious cooperated in this charade by storing her feelings in her stomach. Finally the acid they produced was creating problems that were endangering her health, and under doctors' orders, she went into therapy.

To guarantee that she never slipped up, that she never expressed a taboo emotion, Arlene had labeled anyone who displayed their feelings openly as *weak*. She took pleasure in thinking of herself as *strong*. She believed that she'd be despised if she exhibited an "emotional display."

During a therapy session, Arlene, who was always composed and cool, began to whimper. The whimper steadily grew into a torrent of tears, which try as she might she couldn't stop. She was unprepared for this emotional outburst, and she was very frightened. "I'm losing my mind," she said between sobs. When she calmed down, she assured me over and over that this was not like her. She never cried, especially not in front of anyone.

Arlene's physical health was at stake, and her well-being depended on "dumping" the pain and sadness she'd been collecting and storing for 30 years. But her conscious mind, which dictated her self-image, strongly disapproved of anyone who "broke down." Consequently, Arlene's unconscious waited until it found a safe place—the therapy session—and someone who wouldn't criticize or judge her expression of emotion—her therapist—before it forced her to accept this part of herself. Arlene needed the part of herself she was discovering, but changing her idea of herself from a cool person to an emotional person was something she had to do the hard way.

The change Arlene had to make the hard way forced her to do something she'd never been able to do. For Johnny, changing the hard way meant relinquishing an ability he'd always counted on.

Johnny was the life of the party, the one who made everyone laugh. Johnny believed that it was his *entertainer* cover that made other people like him. He was certain that if he was just himself and exposed what he believed to be his *boring* under cover, others would have no use for him.

In therapy Johnny kept me entertained. He kept the conversation going and never allowed a lapse. But one day, instead of treating me to his characteristic patter, Johnny was silent. When I asked him why, he said he couldn't think of anything to say. When I asked what he was feeling, he said, "Scared to death." I congratulated him on his courage. For Johnny, admitting that he had nothing to say felt like a death sentence.

He was sure, he told me later, "that any minute you would tell me that if I couldn't think of anything to say, I should leave." This silence lasted for weeks, but it occurred only in therapy sessions. On the "outside," Johnny continued to liven up every gathering and was never at a loss for words. But in his sessions Johnny would just sit and squirm and say, "This is foolish, nothing's being accomplished, I should stop coming." He kept repeating that he should stop coming, but every week he showed up. Nothing was being accomplished except that Johnny was taking the biggest risk of his life. He was risking that if he was just himself and *boring*, he'd be abandoned.

Although he was ready to face the danger of being boring, Johnny's conscious mind didn't approve. So when his unconscious took away his words, his conscious rebelled and squirmed and made him uncomfortable. Finally Johnny once again found his tongue, but he was never really the same. He could still tell jokes and entertain, but more and more often—to his great relief—he could also just be quiet and listen.

When you change the hard way you literally change in spite of yourself. One part of you challenges the route that another part of you has chosen. This can make you feel helpless, vulnerable, exposed, and in jeopardy.

OUT OF CONTROL. The best indicator that you're changing the hard way is the sensation of being out of control. This sensation has been described to me by people who are going through it as "how a baby must feel when it's tossed up into the air"; "entering a very dark tunnel and knowing that I have to keep going forward although I have no idea where I'm going or what I'm going to run into"; "going crazy"; and "losing my mind."

We have many expressions to describe this experience— "falling apart," "coming unglued," and "losing it"—to name a few. And then there's the dreaded "breakdown," nervous or otherwise, which is so universally feared. All of these sayings conjure up poor Humpty-Dumpty who couldn't be put together again. They also plainly illustrate what our culture thinks of the experience they describe. Clearly, it's considered awful, terrible, and dangerous—something to be avoided at all costs.

What is actually happening when you experience being out of your own control is that the walls around your self-concept— your idea of yourself—are expanding to include more of you. You're integrating into your total picture of yourself elements of your personality that you previously disowned. Parts of yourself that were once buried in shadow are emerging into light.

Imagine yourself flying along on one or two engines. Suddenly you become aware that a third engine is firing up beneath you. The sudden heat and the unaccustomed rush of power may be disconcerting, or even frightening, but as soon as you get used to it, you wonder how you ever got along without it.

When your conscious mind doesn't recognize how much better your life is going to be when you once again "own" these denied parts of yourself, when it actively resists the change you're getting ready to make, your unconscious mind will take matters into its own hands. This will feel to your conscious mind like being out of control. Feeling out of control can further scare your conscious mind and cause it to begin feeding you the cultural line—that being out of control is bad and dangerous. You may find yourself having thoughts like "Are you crazy?" or "What are you doing?" or even "Get a grip on yourself!"

When Alice came into therapy, the problem she presented was generalized unhappiness and exhaustion. She'd been a nurse, she said proudly, for 20 years. Actually Alice was tired of nursing, but her *dedicated* cover kept her from realizing that she didn't want to do it anymore. All of her self-regard was based on her *dedicated nurse* cover, but she was having trouble making herself get up and go to work.

After six months of therapy during which she'd begun to recognize how much of herself she had to deny to continue nursing, Alice started to fall apart. She would suddenly start to cry at work and once, while attending a professional workshop, she began to cry and tremble uncontrollably. Her colleagues and friends, some of whom were therapists, told her that if she wasn't careful, she'd break down. Alice was terrified. "What's happening to me?" she asked. "Am I going to fall apart completely?"

Alice was changing the hard way. Whether her friends, colleagues, or her own conscious mind liked it or not, Alice was going to demonstrate that there was much more to her than her *dedicated* cover. She was going to accept, integrate, and expose her dreaded under cover capacity to be *selfish*. But it wasn't going to be easy.

Alice was forced to take a leave of absence, something she'd sworn she'd never do. But once she no longer had to go to work, her crying and trembling stopped. She began, to her chagrin, to have a wonderful time. She read and walked and the "generalized unhappiness and exhaustion" that had brought her into therapy vanished. Alice's desire to obey her family's dictum to be the *good one*, the *one who helps and saves*, had kept her from seeing who she really was or exploring what she'd really like to do. Breaking down was her unconscious's way to expand her horizons, to show her options that she was unable to see as long as she worked as a dedicated nurse.

If this is happening to you, if you recognize yourself in my description of changing the hard way, if you feel out of control, you may, like Alice, be resisting the experience of change. You may be afraid. But if this *is* happening to you, don't be afraid, you are not losing yourself—it's much more likely that you're about to regain yourself.

If you're changing the hard way, if you feel like you're coming unglued, losing it, falling apart, or breaking down, this isn't bad news—it's *good* news! You may already know this. You may be able to silence some of the critical and frightened messages coming from your conscious mind. But in our society changing the hard way, which requires losing it, is still criticized and feared, so there's probably a lot of pressure on you—internal and external—not to change.

Sometimes when you're expanding and preparing to incorporate a previously disowned part of yourself, your struggle can remind friends or family members of a denied part of themselves. If they aren't ready to accept their denied part, seeing you in the process of accepting your disowned aspect can be very threatening. They may react to this threat by trying to stop you from changing. They may caution you not to "fall apart" or "break down."

Harry was a passive man who came into therapy to feel better about himself. After six months in therapy, Harry started to "fall apart." He yelled at his business partner, George, and forgot his wife, Pearl's, birthday. George and Pearl, who had always hated each other, joined forces to tell Harry to quit therapy because "it was ruining him."

By that point Harry had gone as far as he was ready to go. He had unbalanced his two most important relationships and was not yet able to risk a further disintegration of his support system. Harry did leave therapy, but he had already changed; his relationships would never be exactly the same.

GETTING HELP. Changing the hard way is what finally brings some people into therapy. They may have been uneasy, unsatisfied, or unhappy before, but now they feel hopeless, desperate, even in danger. It is this shift in the way they feel that brings them into therapy. Nothing in their lives may have changed. They can't point to any reason for their increased discomfort, but what they're feeling has become intolerable. They don't realize it, but they've fallen off the edge or the tip— they're changing the hard way. They often have a stricken look on their face and use one of those expressions to describe what's happening to them. "I'm losing it," they say. "I'm falling apart! I'm not myself." They seem to be saying, "I'm losing myself and if I'm not myself then I don't know who I am or who I'll be. Maybe I'll be someone whom no one will love!"

FALSE PRETENSES. Although clearly in pain and asking for help, people who are changing the hard way rarely come into therapy to make the change their unconscious has launched. They just want to stop this "terrible thing" that's happening to them. They want to get back in control. They want to be themselves again. They may not have liked their *old* self, but now, faced with the possibility of being someone they don't recognize, they want that *old* self back.

Sometimes people don't wait until they're standing in midair to go for help. They seek therapy as soon as they notice a change in the wind. When people come into therapy before the hard change is actually under way, they rarely describe the change their unconscious intends them to make as the problem. Instead, they volunteer as the problem what someone else told them is wrong with them. "My husband says I'm too much of a perfectionist," they'll say, or "My girlfriend says I don't share my feelings." Or else they present a camouflage problem. Nothing tangible may have changed regarding the camouflage problem, but suddenly this problem, which had been annoying, upsetting, or irritating, has become unbearable.

Perhaps you've had this experience: For weeks, months, or even years, you've complained about your dead-end job or your uncommunicative spouse and promised yourself that one day you'd go into therapy. Then one day, you don't really know why, you call a therapist. If your distress over your job or your spouse was camouflage—a real problem but one you couldn't solve until you could face a larger danger—then what has actually changed may have nothing to do with your job or your spouse, but with your *readiness* to face the larger danger. Perhaps you have become ready to make an important change in *yourself*, such as reclaiming an essential part of yourself that you've been forced to live without—to rev up that third engine that you didn't even know was operational. And once you've made *that* change, the camouflage change will be a piece of cake.

THE HAND IN THE FIRE. When people come to see me, presenting what looks like a camouflage problem, I suspect that they may be about to leap into a change that must be made the hard way. I tell them about the growing edge and tip of the diving board. I suggest that the distress they're experiencing may be unrelated to the "problem" they present, and that they may be getting ready to make a change they didn't know they needed to make. I assure them that if they're ready to make this change, they'll probably soon find themselves changing, standing in midair.

When they ask me how to tell if they're ready, I guarantee them that they'll know soon enough. Quite often, after a couple

179

of weeks in therapy, they begin to complain that instead of feeling better, they feel worse. Then I congratulate them on their readiness and explain about the hand in the fire.

Imagine, I say, that your hand is engulfed in flame but your hand is anesthetized. Thanks to the anesthetic, you don't feel any pain but your hand is being damaged. Therapy—when you're ready to endure the consequences—turns off the anesthetic. Suddenly you feel the pain. But you also have an opportunity, sometimes the first of your life, to pull your hand out of the flame and stop the damage.

The important thing to remember about changing the hard way is that while it isn't going to kill you, it *is* probably going to hurt, and sometimes quite a lot. When you're ready to change the hard way, you *will* survive, but when your hand is in the fire—it can be difficult to remember that.

In the last chapter I introduced Lee, whose *dependent* cover forced her to flip back and forth as she tried to separate from her boyfriend, John. Lee had modeled her mother's *dependent* and *incompetent* covers, which her father validated by scaring her with stories of the awful things that might happen to her, belittling her every attempt to take care of herself, and keeping her dependent on his money. Although she was intelligent and talented, Lee believed her *stupid* and *inadequate* covers and thought she couldn't survive alone. Asking John to move out was the most courageous act of her life. It announced to her mother that women didn't have to be dependent on men, and to her father that she didn't need him, or any man, to take care her.

In therapy, Lee was developing her ability to take care of herself. She recognized that under cover she had her father's *self-reliance*, but sometimes when she was alone demons from her past came back to haunt her. At these times she was certain that, like her mother, she couldn't cope on her own; and she was terrified that her father would be mad at her, and punish her.

Sometimes her fear was so great that she'd wake in the night, certain she was having a stroke or a heart attack. It took a year of intense work for Lee to reclaim enough of her *self-sufficient* under cover so that she felt safe enough to be alone most of the time. During this year, Lee saw a lot of me and of her physician, requiring our assurance that she was physically and mentally intact. But it was her own *readiness* that made her able to endure her terrible fear, and finally stop asking John to come back. It was Lee's *readiness* that made her able to survive her terrifying past dangers.

THE FEAR THAT FEELS LIKE DYING. Changes made the hard way are painful and scary and, for many, produce the "fear that feels like dying." When you're changing the hard way you can literally feel as though your *life* is at stake. This terror is what you have been avoiding. This terror is what your unconscious has been protecting you from. But just as it protected you before, your unconscious is protecting you now. If you're changing the hard way—even if it feels as though you're out of control, losing it, or breaking down—if you've found yourself in midair, you're ready to change.

When you're changing the hard way, it's especially important to be kind to yourself, to call a truce in your civil war and use all of your loving and comforting skills to bolster and support yourself. It's also important to avoid critical and judgmental people and to surround yourself, as much as possible, with people who are encouraging and accepting. You need and deserve all the kindness and care you can get. Changing the hard way will be tough enough without self-criticism or judgment.

BUT I WANT TO BE READY

Not everyone who wants to change—not even those who come into therapy—is ready to change. Wanting and trying won't make you able to endure the consequences of the change you want to make. When you can't make a change you want to make, it hurts. But the change you want to make will probably bring a new kind of hurt: catastrophic expectations, feeling out of control, breaking down, having your hand in the flame, the fear that feels like dying. As much as it hurts to stay the way you are, changing—even though you can't see it now—may hurt more. You may hate the old hurt, but you're familiar with it, and you may not know how to deal with the new one. As long as the new hurt promises to be worse than the old, your unconscious will probably make it impossible for you to change.

You can hang around the edge or the tip. You can spend your time and energy trying a method that worked for someone else, keeping your eye on the ball, criticizing yourself, learning all there is to know about your "problem," and practicing self-discipline. But if you're not *ready* to tolerate the pain of the change—as hard as you work to change—your unconscious will work to keep you from changing.

WHEN YOU CAN YOU WILL

Are you standing at the growing edge wanting to do something you've never done before? Have you been trying to prepare yourself for, and guarantee the outcome of, the change you want to make, before you risk it? Unfortunately, the fog surrounding the edge is too thick to see through, and you won't know for sure what awaits below—the consequences of the leap—until you actually make it. You'll be ready to leap when—right or wrong, succeed or fail, rewarded or punished; even if you're rejected, fired, humiliated, or abandoned—*you will survive.*

Maybe you're standing at the tip of the diving board wanting to do something that had terrible consequences the last time you did it. Have you been telling yourself that everything will be all right and resisted thinking about what might go wrong? Denying the consequences of a dive won't eliminate them. You'll be ready to dive when whatever you find in the pool below—pain, fear, sadness, despair, terror, loneliness, or loss—*won't destroy you.*

There may be many things standing between you and the change you can't force yourself to make. But when you're ready to make that change, you will make it, either the easy way or the hard way. And having made it, you'll find that there is a price to pay for it. In the next chapter you'll discover what you can expect to pay for change after you've made it.

The Price
and the Payoff

———

When you're ready to confront and survive your own personal dangers, you will change, but making the change is not the end of the story. You may have been so focused on making the change that you haven't given much thought to its aftermath. But once you have changed, once you've accomplished the thing you wanted to do, look around and you'll probably find that you've paid a "price" for it. It isn't that the change won't bring you the prize you hope for. It may very well bring you exactly what you want. But when it does, the result you desired may also cost you in ways you hadn't anticipated. This chapter describes some of the kinds of bills that come due when you have finally changed.

Sometimes the price is small: getting your driver's license, for example, may turn you into the family chauffeur. Sometimes the price is high: when you buy a house, you may have to keep a job you hate because you can't afford to be out of work. Sometimes you can anticipate the price, and sometimes the price comes as a big surprise.

Before I moved from my parents' home in suburban Queens to a tiny two-room apartment on Manhattan's Upper West Side, my friend Dennis came to spend an afternoon. I chattered on and on about my great adventure, "I will finally be out on my own," I said, "able to create my own space and come and go as I please." Dennis smiled.

"Yes, yes, that's true," he said, "but you won't be living on this quiet pretty street, or," he continued, "have all this good food in the refrigerator," as he finished the leftover roast beef my mom had made the night before.

"Right," I said, "but I won't always have to say where I'm going or be concerned that someone will worry if I'm late!"

Dennis smiled again. "Yes, that's true," he said, "you give and you get."

In its limited vision, your conscious mind may only see the payoff it's hoping to achieve by changing—the get and not the give or the price you'll have to pay for change. If you've been struggling to lose weight, your conscious mind may have told you that once you lose the weight, you'll be loved and desirable. You'll get married, your parents will be proud of you, and everything will be wonderful. This pep talk may make you feel good, but it ignores the fact that once thin you may *still* not be loved by the person you desire. You may finally be as alluring as you hoped you'd be, but be unprepared for the new sexual pressures you have to face. And rather than being proud of you, your parents may be uncomfortable with a thin you.

BETTER SAFE THAN SORRY

Perhaps you think that you're better off not knowing what to expect, that what you don't know won't hurt you. But knowing what to expect can help you prepare for the price when it comes. Here I'll present three different prices that are often the cost of change.

PRICE #1: *The Unachieved Secondary Payoff*
The change you want to make, the one your conscious mind is focused on, is your "primary payoff." But there may be a "secondary payoff," one you don't acknowledge, that you hope will come along for the ride.

PRICE #2: *Breaking the Relationship Contract*
When you make a significant change, you may abandon your "assigned" role and break your relationship contract with one or more important people in your life. Having made the change you wanted to make, you may have to pay the price of losing these relationships.

PRICE #3: *Giving Up the Dream*
Making significant changes in your life may require you to surrender the hope that someone other than yourself will finally solve your problems or make you happy. You may get the thing you want, but at the cost of your dream.

SECONDARY PAYOFF

A change you want to make, such as leaving home, going to college, or finding a lover, is your primary payoff. You may not realize or acknowledge that there's another, secondary, payoff you're also hoping for. Typical secondary payoffs are that the change will bring you happiness, validation, self-confidence, or enhanced self-esteem; or that you will finally feel safe, acceptable, or "normal." Like Stan in the following example, you may have focused so totally on your primary payoff that you don't recognize the existence of your secondary payoff.

Stan came to see me because he was suffering from performance anxiety. He was a comedian who'd been struggling for years and was finally about to get his big break, but he was having trouble remembering his routines and was terrified that he would "crash and burn onstage."

Stan's primary payoff—his acknowledged goal—was to do well in his upcoming engagement. His career was on the line, he assured me. If he bombed, it would be a terrible setback. This was, of course, the truth. But what Stan didn't say, and in fact

187

didn't know, was that there was a secondary payoff that he wanted equally as much as, if not more than, the primary one. Stan's identity was riding on his career as a comic.

As a child Stan had an *invisible* cover. His father left the family shortly after he was born and his mother found a boyfriend with whom she was so busy that there was no time for baby Stan. Until the sixth grade Stan dutifully acted out his *invisible* cover, feeling left out and always walking home from school alone. One day Stan's teacher convinced him to tell jokes in the talent show. Overnight Stan had an identity; he was the class comic. From that moment on he believed that his *visibility* depended on his performance—he was either a *comic* or he was *invisible*. Consequently, in his upcoming engagement he had too much at stake. Stan was risking not just this performance, or even his career, but his identity.

Performing was one of Stan's greatest pleasures, but he couldn't think about how much fun he was going to have because all he could think was, "God, don't let me forget my lines. Don't let me go back to being invisible." Before Stan could get onstage, enjoy his performance, and do his very best, he had to know that if the worst happened and he bombed, he'd still be *somebody*—that he'd survive and go on.

Stan had been putting all of his energy into memorization techniques and rehearsal, but these techniques weren't working. In therapy he recognized that his secondary motivation for succeeding as a comic was to be *seen* and *valued*. He began to direct his attention to appreciating his value as separate and distinct from his ability or success as a comic. As his personal self-regard grew, Stan began to feel that less and less was actually going to be at stake in his forthcoming performance. As a result, Stan not only found it increasingly easy to remember his routine, he remembered how much he enjoyed performing and began to look forward to the performance.

Anyone who saw Jimmy Connors compete in the 1991 U.S. Tennis Open saw an athlete who wasn't being distracted by an unacknowledged secondary payoff. Jimmy's primary payoff—to play tennis—was uppermost in his mind. No one watching could doubt how much he wanted to win; but even more than he wanted to win, Jimmy wanted to play. Celebrating his 39th birthday on Center Court, he was well past what should have been his prime as a tennis player, and many believed he shouldn't have been there at all. Because nothing else was on the line—losing wasn't too big a price for him to pay—he wasn't distracted. He not only played, he was his very best self, and enjoyed himself as well.

Chances are, the change *you* want to make won't require you to tell jokes to hundreds of people or play championship tennis on Center Court. But whatever primary payoff you desire—quitting your job, confronting your brother about incest, making dinner for your mother-in-law, or asking the pretty neighbor out for coffee—there may be a secondary payoff you can't afford to forfeit, but which you haven't acknowledged.

BE CAREFUL WHAT YOU WISH FOR ... As I have said, as long as you're not ready to confront and survive the danger that attends the change you want to make, your unconscious will keep you from making it. But sometimes events that are out of your control can conspire to give you what you want before you're ready to pay the price it will demand.

If you achieve your primary payoff, but not your secondary payoff, the success that you thought would thrill and delight you may be unexpectedly empty. This is why even when you get exactly what you think you want, you can be disappointed.

Vicki's primary payoff was for people to love her songs. The unrecognized secondary payoff was her belief that the applause of an audience would prove to her family and herself that she wasn't a *flake*. She'd worked for many years trying to get her songs published and recorded and herself "discovered," but had very little actual success. Then, an old friend who'd always loved her music offered to produce "An Evening with Vicki." He rented a nightclub and created the perfect atmosphere for the invitation-only performance. The evening was perfect. Vicki had it just the way she wanted it. She was superb, and the audience response was all she could have hoped for. But when the evening was over, and her adrenaline returned to normal, she couldn't stop thinking, "God, it isn't enough!"

The primary payoff of success and the approval of others, which both Stan and Vicki wanted so desperately, can feel great. But if, in your secret heart, you suspect—as they did—that you're flawed, inadequate, or inferior, and you're hoping that the change you make will also

- correct your flaw,
- validate your worth,
- shore up your leaky self-image,
- undo the damage of the past,
- rewrite a cover, or
- make an under cover quality acceptable,

you will almost certainly be disappointed.

External success cannot heal internal wounds. This has been the painful public lesson learned by so many of our most brilliant, talented, funny, and charismatic people. Lenny Bruce, Marilyn Monroe, John Belushi, Freddie Prinze, Judy Garland, James Dean, Janis Joplin, Richard Pryor, and countless others skyrocketed from the depths of a poor, weird, flake, or loser cover to the rarefied heights of fame, fortune, and acclaim. If they expected the success, applause, money, and accomplishment to bring them the secondary payoff of feeling valuable, acceptable, lovable, or safe, they were almost certainly disappointed.

This brings us again to the awesome power wielded by your cover story. Until it's safe for you to recognize that you're more than just the person you pretended to be for the sake of your family balance, the entire world can stand up and applaud, and it won't mean a thing.

Most of us never have to face this dilemma. We can keep alive the fantasy that if only we were smarter, prettier, richer, more famous, talented, or taller, we would be loved, admired, respected; and feel good, safe, or whole. But fabulous success steals this fantasy and reveals it as the sham it really is. The celebrated individuals I mentioned above reaped all of the primary payoffs that our society can offer, but these couldn't bring them the more important secondary payoffs they were hoping for. Worse, the achievement of one cost them the fantasy of the other. Who can blame them if they despaired of ever feeling what they longed to feel? Who can blame them for giving up hope?

In his 1991 interview with David Frost, Elton John said he was "lucky to be alive." In that candid and courageous interview, John described perfectly the dilemma of receiving your primary payoff but not your secondary payoff. John said that he'd always felt like the unwanted little boy his dad had abandoned. For the five years it took for him to ascend from "nobody" to "superstar," he was able to relish his unexpected good fortune. But, surprisingly, he found that once he'd clearly "made it," having it all didn't make him feel any more deserving.

The dichotomy between *what he had* and *what he thought he deserved* was too vast. All of his success simply highlighted his inadequacy.

He described his attempts to ease the pain of having so much and feeling like so little. He detailed an existence in which he abused substances and people alike, an existence that nearly killed him. Then, with the help of a substance-abuse program, he recognized that before he could benefit from his success, he had to feel deserving. He worked to achieve his secondary payoff and is now able to relax and enjoy the wonderful rewards his talent has brought him.

EXERCISE—*When Then . . .*

What is your secondary payoff? What is it that you secretly hope to achieve by making a fortune, having a baby, or learning to drive a car? Are you also hoping to be independent, prove you can take care of someone else, or feel like an adult? One can make a fortune and still not be independent; have a baby and still not feel like a caretaker; and learn to drive without feeling like a grown-up.

If you don't easily recognize your secondary payoff, you might find it by filling in the When, Then blank. Get a long piece of paper and a pen. At the top of the page write WHEN I GET _____ THEN I'LL BE _____. Write as long a list as you can. Some of the adjectives my clients often use are: *happy, loved, understood, important, appreciated, safe, comfortable, right, vindicated,* and *sexy,* but you may have an entirely different list. When you have your answer, you'll most likely have the secondary payoff you hope your primary payoff will bring you. If you suspect that your primary payoff may not ensure you of your secondary payoff, you might want to think about reordering your priorities, focusing for a while directly on achieving your secondary payoff. When you've separated the two, you may even find that the primary payoff that has been eluding you is suddenly easier to achieve.

Do you believe that these secondary payoffs—feeling loved, appreciated, valued, and deserving—must come to you from outside yourself, from your loved ones? If so, your relationships with these people may be too important, and a change that risks these relationships may turn out to be a surprisingly unpleasant price for you to pay.

BREAKING THE RELATIONSHIP CONTRACT

In chapter 2, I described the relationship contract, an unwritten and unacknowledged but binding contract between you and anyone with whom you have a relationship, including family members, friends, or colleagues. This contract describes the basis of the relationship, the role each person will play, and stipulates that for the life of the relationship, neither will change their assigned role. When you make difficult changes, you may find that you've changed in ways that break some of your relationship contracts. You may find that you're no longer the person you were when you entered into contracts with many of the most important people in your life.

The relationship contract keeps the balance between people firm. If you break the contract, you unbalance the relationship. If, for example, you're an alcoholic, many of your relationships may be based on your self-destructive or dependent behavior. You may play the role of the *weak* one, while the other person plays the role of the *strong* one. If, after years of alcoholic drinking, you finally get clean and sober, the relationship contract—in which you agreed to abuse your body and jeopardize your health and safety, while the other agreed to worry, caution, complain, or bully—is broken.

Your relationship becomes unbalanced. You may have bickered and complained about each other throughout your relationship, but it always felt right. When you change it will no longer feel right, and you will no longer "fit." If you have changed, but the other has not changed—if they still want or need to worry, bully, or complain—the basis for your relationship with them is no longer there.

When you change and break a relationship contract, the relationship itself must change. There are several ways this can happen:

OPTION #1:

You change and the other person changes in a complementary way. Together you establish a new balance and draw up a new relationship contract. Steve and Alan, the brothers I mentioned in chapter 2 who joined forces to help each other abandon their respective family roles, are a good example of how two people can change and establish a new contract. In their old relationship contract Alan was *scornful* and Steve was *jealous*. In their new relationship contract, which is based on respect and support, both are interested and helpful.

This option, in which both people change and create a new and mutually rewarding relationship contract, is the ideal, but not the only, outcome of a change that breaks a relationship contract.

OPTION #2:

In this option you change, and not only doesn't the other person change, he or she denies that you have changed. Gerri, whose story you read in chapter 2, found out that even when you make dramatic changes, other people may continue to see and treat you as they always have. Gerri's family didn't recognize that she'd lost 50 pounds and continued to treat her as if she were someone whose eating habits had to be monitored.

It's uncomfortable for the person who's changed when the other person ignores their change and doggedly continues to play out the old relationship contract. But many people like Gerri, who want to stay in touch with their families, choose to endure the discomfort of the imbalance. For them the relationship isn't what it once was, but the participants remain in contact.

OPTION #3:

In this option you change, the other person recognizes that you've changed, but he or she can't change in a way that would reestablish balance in the relationship. Both people become very uncomfortable with each other. There may be a period of tug-of-war, during which one or both try to find some way to make the relationship feel right so it can continue. Sometimes people pretend for a while that nothing has changed; sometimes they squabble or accuse one another of betrayal or unfairness. Others can be drawn into the fray. Mutual friends can try to mediate or bring someone back into line. But in the end, if you and the other person can't find a way to ignore the discomfort and continue the relationship, or establish a new contract, one or the other will usually break off the contact. This can come as the result of a blow-out, or simply by someone slipping away.

An example of this can be seen in a classic marriage between an alcoholic and an enabler. These marriages, while perfectly balanced, are often stormy, with each person trying to change the other. But the relationships usually remain intact as long as both continue to play their roles. It is when the alcoholic gets sober, or the enabler stops enabling, that these relationships fall apart. Often, the unchanged partner immediately seeks someone to play out the role the old partner abandoned.

DON'T BREAK THAT CONTRACT. Because the loss of your most important relationships can be too big a price to pay for the change you want to make, the internal pressure not to make a change that endangers a relationship contract is very great. Many people, like Denise in the following example, sacrifice essential parts of their lives in order to maintain relationship contracts that were established in childhood. Denise desperately wanted to revitalize her career, but not at the expense of her relationship with her older brother, Jed. That was too big a price to pay.

At 21 Denise had a promising acting career and seemed headed for stardom. Then, suddenly, she couldn't do anything right. She heard rumors that she was difficult to work with. Directors who'd loved her work stopped hiring her. Finally her agent fired her. At 30 she was living in a tiny apartment, driving an old car, and working in a shoe store.

When Denise came to see me, she was desperate. She didn't understand what had happened and couldn't figure out what to do about it. She spent most of her time brutally criticizing herself for every move she made or didn't make and for every thought she had. She was paralyzed by her self-criticizing civil war.

Denise didn't consciously realize that her success threatened her relationship with her brother, Jed. Almost ten years older, Jed had always been her "white knight," protecting Denise from their father's rages when they were children. Now he provided moral and financial support for her struggle. As long as Denise was in trouble, Jed could come to her rescue. Her struggle maintained the bond they had forged so many years ago, and neither knew what their relationship would be if she didn't need him.

In therapy, I explained the relationship contract to Denise. She drew her family pie and realized that by failing in her career she was just living up to her contract with Jed— confirming her *dependent*, and his *caretaker*, covers. She saw that because her relationship with Jed began when she was a little girl, there was no room in it for the adult she wanted to become.

Recognizing that failing was her way of protecting her brother and her relationship with him changed Denise's idea of herself. Instead of seeing herself as a failure, she accepted herself as the loving and grateful sibling she was. She broke the cycle of self-criticism and stopped beating herself up for her failures. She brought Jed into therapy with her to work on establishing a new balance, a new relationship contract. Today Denise and Jed's relationship contract is much more an alliance of equals, and Denise is once again seriously pursuing her career.

Denise was lucky. She and Jed, like Alan and Steve above, were able to change in ways that enabled them to maintain their relationships. But often this is not the case. I have frequently seen people who have been close family members or "best friends"—people who genuinely feel the loss of each other, and profoundly want their relationship to continue—who just can't make the kinds of complementary changes that would make a continuing relationship possible.

Over and over I've seen people make essential changes in their life and find that they've inadvertently broken a relationship contract, which costs them a significant relationship.

I've seen people lose weight, become successful, or get married and have their loved ones go on treating them as though they were still fat, unsuccessful, or lonely. You may very well receive the payoff you want, but it may cost you relationships with friends, relatives, lovers, or children.

You can't predict who will and who won't be able to mesh with the new you. When you make a significant change in your life, you risk losing those people who have been the most important to you. This is a very heavy price to pay for whatever payoff you're hoping to receive. If there's a change you want to make, even if your friends and loved ones have supported and encouraged this change, the price you may have to pay for it, the give for the get, may be the loss of these very same people.

And that brings me to "giving up the dream." The *dream* is the belief that those secondary payoffs, the certainty that you are important, valuable, cherished, safe, lovable, and deserving, can come to you only from outside yourself. As long as you believe in this dream, you can't risk paying the price of losing your primary relationships, and that effectively blocks you from making certain changes in your life.

GIVING UP THE DREAM

Giving up the dream is the hardest price to pay for change. Changes that require you to give up the dream demand that you take responsibility for your own happiness, a burden that you may not yet be able to assume. Giving up the dream means becoming the one who fills up the empty place inside, the one who makes you feel loved and safe.

You may believe that you shouldn't have to do this for yourself. You may believe that if you have to provide the love and comfort you need for yourself, there's something wrong with you. You may believe popular culture, which through the media says that if you were lovable, surely someone else would love you.

Giving up the dream that someone else will finally do what your parents failed to do—give you the feeling of love and security that you need and deserve to feel—runs counter to the deeply ingrained cultural myth that "someday my prince/princess will come" and fix everything. Popular songs, movies, TV shows, fairy tales, and the advice of friends and family all spread the same message: Love will save your life, so go out and get someone to love you.

LIFE'S FOUNDATION. Love and safety *are* the foundation on which lives are built. If you have a solid foundation, if you feel loved and safe, you can pursue your life fully. On your foundation of love you can build relationships, friendships, marriages, or parenthood. On your foundation of safety you can build ideas, creations, businesses, careers, or a life's work. While having a foundation won't guarantee the success of the structures you build, it will guarantee that you have someplace to build them, and if they fall down you have somewhere to start building again.

If you don't feel loved or safe, you're missing an essential part of life's foundation. If you don't have this foundation, you can't risk any kind of building. Even the things of which you are already capable, things for which you have the skills, intelligence, talent, or strength, present too big a risk. You always have to check the foundation. You always have to shore it up. And if you ignore your lack of foundation and try to build anyway, your buildings won't last. If, for example, you feel unlovable, you won't believe that anyone loves you even when they do; and if you feel unsafe, you'll be so busy looking over your shoulder every minute that you'll make building mistakes.

Whether you've thought about it in this way or not, you know if you have a foundation on which to build your life. You know if you feel loved or unloved, safe or unsafe. And you know that having a foundation is not a luxury, it's a necessity. The popular songs are right in their way, when they say that love will save your life. They're just wrong about where this love comes from.

LOOKING FOR LOVE IN ALL THE WRONG PLACES. The chances are that you've been wasting your time looking to others to supply the love and security you need. When you were a child, your parents were your mirror. It was through them that you knew yourself. You decided who *you* were by observing how *they* saw and treated you. Your identity, value, and worth were based on their reaction to you. If they beamed at you, if their arms were warm and welcoming; if, when you looked into their eyes, you saw a wonderful and cherished someone reflected there, then you recognized that you were wonderful and deserved to be cherished. You felt loved and safe. If you felt loved and safe as a child, you feel loved and safe as an adult—you have this essential foundation on which to build your life.

If, however, your parents were cold or distant; if you felt unwanted, a burden; if you were neglected or abused, you may have made the mistake of thinking that this treatment reflected your worth—that you were flawed, inadequate, bad, and unworthy of care. You felt unloved and unsafe. If you felt

199

unloved and unsafe as a child, you feel unloved and unsafe as an adult—you don't have your basic foundation.

Because this feeling of love and safety should have come from *outside you* when you were a child, you may believe that as an adult you can also receive it from an outside source. You may be relentlessly pursuing the dream that the love of another or the validation of the world will supply your missing foundation.

But, as an adult, your foundation—the feeling of being loved and safe—can't come from outside you. It simply can't be provided for you by another person. *This love must come from you.*

As long as you believe that you can be *made* to feel loved or safe by someone or something outside yourself; as long as you hope to receive this from the perfect lover or spouse, an adoring child, your parents' approval, success, awards, applause, wealth, achievement, or anything else—you will be disappointed.

FINDING THE SOURCE. The difficulty you have finding a career, leaving a marriage, or committing to a lover may well be connected to your reluctance to abandon the hope that someone will take this awful problem out of your hands, that someone will do what your parents were unable to do: love you and take care of you.

Taking your life in your own hands means taking it out of anyone else's. Before you can make the difficult change you've been struggling to make, you may have to give up the dream that someone will come along and do it for you.

Giving up the dream is essential, not only to the change you want to make, but to whatever comfort and happiness you wish to have in life. But although it's essential, it isn't easy to do. In fact, it's a kind of catch-22. Before you can love yourself, you must recognize that you're someone who deserves to be loved. Do you think about yourself as someone who deserves to be loved? Do you treat yourself as someone who deserves to be loved? Do you treat yourself as you would treat a lover—the person whose love you believe will save you? Probably not.

If you don't, it's because as a child you mistakenly believed that you were unworthy of love. Consequently, a part of you is damaged and needs to be healed. You can be the one who heals your own damaged part. You can be the one who loves you enough, and you can give up the dream.

Many people, having been disappointed by parents, friends, or lovers, turn to a therapist in the hope that he or she will provide their missing foundation. While therapy can help *you* become the person who loves and cares for yourself, and a therapist can provide nurturing, encouragement, reassurance, and support, a therapist cannot become your source.

Georgia came to see me because she was "always scared." There were so many things she wanted to do, she said, but her fear kept her from trying. A gentle, soft-spoken young woman, she was emotionally fragile and easily moved to tears. Georgia's mother had suffered from violent mood swings and her father, overwhelmed by his role as breadwinner and the needs of his erratic wife, had been unable to protect Georgia from her mother's unexplained rages. As a small child she learned that the world was not a safe place and that to be safe she must do as little as possible.

In therapy Georgia began to build her own foundation. She rediscovered many of the strengths and resources she'd had to bury during a childhood in which it was too dangerous to practice them. Whenever she got too frightened, however, she called me for reassurance.

One evening Georgia called very distraught. After a brief conversation I invited her to come in for a session the following morning at 9:00 A.M. In the middle of the night I developed a terrible intestinal flu. At 7:00 A.M. I dragged myself from bed and called my answering service to ask them to call Georgia and cancel our appointment. They told me that she'd already called to cancel. I went back to bed.

My office was in my home, so when Georgia arrived (she'd actually called to *confirm* not cancel our 9:00 A.M. appointment) and rang the buzzer, I heard her. Again I dragged myself from bed. In my red flannel nightshirt and blue wool knee socks, I'm sure that I looked half dead; I had trouble just standing in the doorway of my office. As briefly as possible I explained the situation to Georgia and promised to call her as soon as I could. I went back to bed.

I was sick for several days. When I was sufficiently recovered I called Georgia to see if she wanted a session. She said she could wait until our scheduled session the following week. When she arrived for that session, I noticed a difference in her. She talked happily about a party she'd attended and a new friend she'd made. There were no tears. Finally I asked Georgia if she, too, was aware of a change. "Last week when I came to see you," she said, "I felt like I was carrying this big bag of garbage. I wanted to give it to you but I saw that you couldn't take it. At first I was angry at you and then I thought, oh well, I'll just have to do something with it myself. Suddenly I knew that I could take care of it myself and since then I've felt much better."

After that, Georgia's life took off. As she risked more and more new experiences, her calls to me became more and more infrequent and then stopped. Finally she stopped therapy altogether. She had given up the hope that someone else would carry her pain and soothe her sadness. She had seen that even I, with the best of intentions, could fail her. She'd learned that other people could not be trusted with the job of loving her, that that was a job she had to do for herself.

It is important to remember that in therapy Georgia had already developed many of the skills she would need to be her own source. That when she took the risk, she was really ready, so if you can't do it right this minute, rather than criticizing yourself once again for something you can't do, reward yourself for how hard you try. Give yourself a present. Trust yourself, because believe it or not, When You Can You Will.

In the
Meanwhile

This has been a book about the process of change. Its message is that although you can't always see how you're doing it, you're always making the most self-protective choices possible. You are always, consciously or unconsciously, acting in your best interests. You can trust yourself.

The idea that you can trust yourself is both tempting and frightening. It's comforting to think that you can like and appreciate yourself just as you are. It's nice to think that you can stop disliking or harassing yourself, stop worrying about what you're not. But this idea that you can appreciate yourself just as you are can be frightening, too. What if I'm wrong? What if you do stop struggling, start enjoying yourself, and never make the change you have in mind?

I believe that you *can't* do what you can't do, and that no amount of worrying, self-criticism, or willpower will help you make a change you're not ready to make. I believe that if there's a change you very much want to make, one that is encouraged and supported by all of your friends and family; one that you believe will enhance your life, or put an end to your pain and suffering; and you've given it your best shot but you simply cannot make it; *there's a good reason that you can't make it!*

Of course your conscious mind may, at this very moment, be reminding you of all the good reasons you have *for* making this change. A friend may be telling you that you can do it all and do it now or that if you can't, you must! Maybe, while you've been reading this book, you have vacillated between hoping I'm right and hoping I'm wrong. Perhaps you've swung back and forth between the relief of recognizing that you can't do what you can't do, and the terror of thinking that no matter what I say, if you can't change right now there's something terribly wrong with you. *There's nothing wrong with you!*

No amount of willpower will alter this fact: As long as dangers that you cannot survive coexist with the change you want to make, you won't be able to make it.

The major source of your personal barriers to change is your original family. Directly or indirectly, but in no uncertain terms, your parents taught you who you had to be and what you could expect from the world. Following the directions they received from their own families, your parents passed on to you the world as it had been given to them, and the world you inherited from your parents is largely the one you inhabit today. If your parents posted detour signs, you avoid that territory, even if it's a place that, as an adult, you really want to visit. If they put bars on your windows, you may not even notice that the doors are wide open. The map they drew for you, which decreed where it was safe and where it was hazardous for you to travel, is the map you still follow. Seeing that others follow different blueprints or venture into different territories won't make you more able to seek alternative paths. Before you can trade in the map you inherited for a newer, updated version, you must trace back the origin of your family's particular map.

You can't learn how to make the change you want to make by observing how others have changed. The road to your change runs directly through you. You must turn your search-light on your past and your present. You must research yourself, looking for the patterns that repeat over and over again in your life and in the lives of your family members.

Human beings do not act in haphazard or contradictory ways; our actions make sense. If you're acting in a way you don't understand, there is a reason, there is an explanation. If you

204

don't, at this moment, know the reason, it is probably because your unconscious is keeping it a protected secret.

Think of yourself as an intricate puzzle, some of whose pieces have been placed out of sight. You don't understand some of your actions, because you can't see all of the pieces. When you do see the missing pieces, you'll understand why you've been acting in this puzzling and perhaps disquieting way. If you search, identify patterns, and keep track of the small pieces you find that don't seem to fit anywhere, when it's safe you'll be able to see the whole, or at least most of your puzzle. And behaviors that now seem contradictory will make sense.

FLYING IN THE FACE OF IT

There's so much pressure on us to ignore our pasts, deny our feelings, intuitions, and instincts, and focus instead on wanting and trying. It's no wonder we're so good at denial. We need it. When we're really in touch with who we are, where we come from, what we need, and what scares us, we run the risk of being at odds with the larger society, which routinely discounts or ridicules these discoveries.

While I was writing this book, Gloria Steinem's book *Revolution from Within* was published and it received at least one review that confirms the larger society's contempt for self-discovery. It attacked Ms. Steinem for what it called her "true confessions." The reviewer didn't want to know about Ms. Steinem's pain and suffering, and was furious at the exposure of her emotional dirty linen. The reviewer was insulted that this respected feminist chose to tell the world that her childhood was painful and brutalizing, that she disliked herself, suffered, made mistakes, and struggled to find a way to heal the scars of that childhood. Why couldn't she go on pretending, like the rest of us? Why couldn't she keep her secrets to herself?

I think that it's precisely because she takes her position as a feminist role model seriously that Ms. Steinem felt compelled to expose her struggle. With real courage, she dared to fly in the face of the conventional wisdom. Can you do as much?

- Can you identify the role you were assigned in your original family?

- Can you see how cleverly you've re-created the balance that existed in that family with your current family—friends, lovers, colleagues, and so on?

- Do you know who you modeled and who you anti-modeled? Are there qualities belonging to a disowned parent that you'd like to have today?

- Did you draw your family pie? Were you able to identify any of the qualities you'd been denied for the sake of your family's balance?

- Have you "blown" your own cover and begun to discover some of the qualities you've been hiding under cover?

- Do you recognize the past or future dangers that lurk in the waters below your growing edge or diving board?

- Have you noticed that there's an emotion missing from your emotional repertoire?

- Have you spontaneously recalled a painful memory from your childhood, or begun to think in a new way about an event you have always remembered?

- Are you willing to consider that the change you can't make today might be connected to a lesson you learned or an experience you had many years ago?

LOOK MA, NO HANDS

Recognizing the existence of your unconscious mind as an active and beneficial participant in your life will make your life much easier. Instead of feeling that you—that is, your conscious mind—must always be on the alert, you can learn to trust your unconscious, relax, and enjoy much more of your life. When you make Freudian slips or convenient mistakes, experience the wandering mind, or behave like someone you don't know, you will understand that these aren't foolish errors or signs of senility, but rather the intentional orchestrations of your unconscious mind working to protect you. And this recognition will change your self-image. Exploring your unconscious's use of camouflage in your life—its misdirection of your attention to problems that cannot be solved, its hiding of feelings and memories in your body, and its burying nuggets of knowledge deep inside your dreams—can provide you with invaluable sources of information you may never have known existed.

Imagine a life in which you don't have to worry quite so much because you *know* not only that you're doing all that you can do but also that when you can do more, you will. Recognizing the power of your unconscious and the contribution it makes to your daily life is one of the best ways I know of to achieve this.

When you do trust that you're doing all that you can do, you won't waste any more precious time or energy trying to be someone you're not, or trying to do something you can't do. You'll no longer emulate someone else's notion of what it means to be "normal," "healthy," "correct," or "good." You'll no longer try to "know better," discipline or criticize yourself, or use anyone else's one-size-fits-all solution. You'll be able just to relax, enjoy yourself, and prepare for the time when you become ready to change.

READY OR NOT, YOU WILL CHANGE

Readiness is that state in which you know that you will survive whatever repercussions you may encounter when you change. When you're ready, you will change. Judging whether you are or are not ready is easy: if you're changing, you're ready; if you're not, you're not. Readiness guarantees that you will change, but not whether it will be the easy way or the hard way.

The easy changes are effortless. Without a struggle, you will make a seamless transition that even you may not recognize until long after you've made it. The easy changes just happen. It isn't the seriousness of your commitment or your intention that makes such change possible, but rather something that seems to be out of your control. Such is the mystery of the easy change.

The only downside to changing the easy way is that you may not trust that the change will last. After all, could anything this easy be for real? The good news is that you don't have to believe in the change to maintain it. So relax and enjoy it.

Changes made the hard way are bumpy, sometimes quite painful, and even terrifying. If you've changed the hard way, or are in the process of changing the hard way, you can testify to the appropriateness of its name. These changes often require that you "blow" your cover, expose an under cover quality, unbalance an important relationship, experience a taboo emotion, or relive a traumatic event. These are the changes you have put off, resisted, denied, and run from most of your life. Having to admit to the family that loves you for being *good* that you are also *bad* may not seem like a big deal, but when you believe that your life depends on their love, and that their love depends on your being good, letting them know the "awful" truth about yourself may be too dangerous and not worth any change.

When you change the hard way, you may suffer from having *your hand in the flame*, which, as we've learned, means enduring a pain you've denied for a lifetime. Or you may experience *the fear that feels like dying*, which you'll recall is the expectation that this change will cost you the love on which you believe your life depends. *The hand in the flame* and *the fear that feels like dying* are terrible in and of themselves, but for many people this distress is exacerbated by the reaction of others.

Remember that our culture judges sadness, pain, and fear as weakness and tries to get us to "hide it away." Consequently, it's not only what's happening to you that makes the hard changes so hard, but the fact that these changes quite often bring out the worst in your friends and family. It is from loved ones that you are most likely to hear the cautionary, "What's the matter with you?" or "Get a grip on yourself," or even "Better be careful, if you keep this up you'll break down."

Breaking down, losing it, or falling apart are much to be feared and avoided in our culture. Unfortunately, many of the hard changes cannot be made without these experiences. And ironically, it is precisely the fact that the old you is coming apart that will allow the new you to come together.

If you're worried that you're losing it; if you start crying for "no reason"; if you're scared or angry a lot of the time; if you can't get an event from your childhood out of your mind; if your usual functioning has been interrupted; if friends, relatives, or co-workers are "worried about you": you're probably changing the hard way. And if you are, *go get help*. You don't have to endure this alone. You deserve to have support as you struggle to emerge into yourself. You deserve to know

- that you're perfectly normal;
- that what's happening to you is the good news, not the bad;
- that this *is* the way people make the hard changes;
- that it won't last forever;
- that you *will* survive, and go on to have a much happier life than you ever had before.

Even if you believe what I just said, when you change the hard way, you won't be able to hold on to this knowledge. No one can! You'll forget and need to be reminded. Find someone to remind you, someone to see you through the difficult period

209

of changing the hard way. Call a therapist, a peer-counseling group, a general-support group, a sympathetic and accepting friend, or an anonymous program.

THE GIVE FOR THE GET

If you have finally changed either the easy or the hard way, you already know that virtually no significant change comes without its price. Did you achieve your primary payoff, but not your secondary payoff? Did you divorce your husband or get a graduate degree, only to discover that you still feel inadequate? Did you stop taking care of your family at the expense of your health, only to discover that you'd broken a contract and lost an important relationship? Or did you change in a way that enhanced your self-regard and made you a stronger person, only to find that you had to give up the dream?

DREAMING A NEW DREAM

To all of us, being loved means being safe, and being unloved feels like a death sentence. If you believe that you must be loved by another, and that in order to be loved by that other, you must be—or appear to be—someone you're not, changing will be too dangerous. When the change you want to make threatens to "blow" your cover or expose you as someone they won't love, you won't be able to make such a change until you can give up the dream—the mistaken belief that someone other than yourself can and will make you feel loved and safe.

It is only when you are able to love yourself, when your security does not depend on the approval or acceptance of another person, that you will be able to make this change.

Perhaps you're thinking, "But there's no problem, I want to be the person 'they' want me to be. I want to get a good job, and 'they' want me to get a good job." When everyone agrees that you should make this change and still you can't make it, suspect the possibility that, even if you can't see how, making this change will expose you as someone you're not supposed to be—someone "they" won't love. And that before you can make this change, you will have to give up the dream.

THE ROCK AND THE HARD PLACE

Regrettably, for adults, this dream—that someone else can fill up the empty place inside you and make you feel whole and safe—is an illusion. It doesn't work. *You* must be the source of your security. Your safety depends on your loving yourself, because as long as you imagine that your safety depends on someone else's continuing love, you can't afford to risk losing it or them.

Your need to feel safe, however, is not an illusion. We all need to feel safe; that is the foundation on which we build our lives. But no matter how good it feels in the short run, the love or approval of another is not a true foundation. You *can* and *must* be the one who loves you. You *can* and *must* be the master builder of your own foundation. But how?

YES VIRGINIA, THERE REALLY IS
AN INNER CHILD

Growing up requires each of us to pass through various developmental stages. At each stage certain conditions must be present if we are to successfully complete our developmental tasks. For example, you will learn to trust only if, when you're dependent and helpless, your environment is safe and secure. You learn independence only if, when you're ready to chance separation, your parents are able to let you go. If you reach a developmental stage and the conditions aren't right, a part of you doesn't develop—you don't learn to trust, or be independent. A part of you remains the age it was when your development was interrupted. This is what is meant by the "inner child."

If, as a child, you didn't learn to trust or to be independent, there will be behaviors that, as an adult, you won't be able to accomplish—anything that requires trust or independence. Fortunately, that "child" still lives inside of you, and it's still possible to correct the error of your childhood, to create the conditions under which the developmental stage can be completed, and to have that happy childhood.

Creating the conditions under which a part of yourself can move through a missed developmental stage may require you to think about and treat yourself in unfamiliar ways. You may have to treat yourself in exactly the opposite way that your family treated you. You may have to love and accept yourself unconditionally, and this may be the opposite of what you believe you deserve. You may not get much support from your family, friends, or the culture at large. The work of becoming the one who loves you is often derided or dismissed by much of our society, but there are many books currently being written on the subject, and many workshops that specialize in teaching techniques you can use to accomplish it. If you're ready to accept the challenge of becoming the one who loves you, experience it. You should have no trouble finding help.

IN THE MEANWHILE

As a teacher of mine said about the process of self-discovery, "It's a lifetime job, and the only hurry is to start." So if you've started; if you've begun to consider that you might really be a self-protective person who's doing the best that he or she can; if you've had the courage to explore some of the lessons and messages of your childhood, with an eye toward un-covering; if now and then you catch yourself in an awful self-criticism and are able to turn it into a statement of glowing self-regard; if you lose your keys, forget where you're going, make an embarrassing slip of the tongue, or do something you really wish you hadn't done, and instead of getting upset, you giggle—you're on your way.

And in the meanwhile focus on the joy and pleasure that is available to you right now:

- go to the movies,
- get a massage,
- take a bubble bath,
- have a cup of tea,
- have a tea party,
- or a slumber party,
- call or visit a friend,
- cook spaghetti sauce,
- hold a puppy,
- stick your toes in the ocean,
- write a love letter,
- sleep late,
- walk in the mountains,
- have a picnic,
- have a gourmet lunch,
- have a hot dog with everything on it.

Make up your own list of pleasures and then allow yourself to experience them. Don't put off enjoying your life until it and you are exactly what you think they should be. For just this moment, accept yourself as you are, because you can't do what you can't do, and WHEN YOU CAN, YOU WILL.

Bibliography

Adams, James. *Conceptual Blockbusting*. New York: W. W. Norton, 1974.

Allport, Gordon W. *Becoming: Basic Considerations for a Psychology of Personality*. Binghamton, New York: Yale University Press, 1955.

Bateson, Gregory. *Mind and Nature: A Necessary Unity*. New York: E. F. Hutton.

Bloomfield, Harold, with Leonard Felder. *Making Peace With Your Parents*. New York: Ballantine Books, 1983.

Bowen, Murray. *Family Therapy and Clinical Practice*. New York: J. Aronson, 1978.

Buscaglia, Leo F. *Living, Loving, and Learning*. New York: Ballantine Books, 1982.

Campbell, Joseph. *The Hero with a Thousand Faces*. New Jersey: Princeton University Press, 1949.

de Castillejo, Claremont Irene. *A Feminine Psychology*. New York: Doubleday, 1988.

Erickson, Milton. *Hypnotic Realities*. New York: Irvington Publishers, 1976.

Erickson, Milton. *Hypnotherapy: An Exploratory Casebook*. New York: Irvington Publishers, 1979.

Friedman, Marsha. *Overcoming the Fear of Success*. New York: Warner Books, 1980.

Freud, Sigmund. *The Psychopathology of Everyday Life*. New York: W. W. Norton, 1965.

Gallwey, Timothy W. *Inner Tennis*. New York: Random House, 1976.

Gillis, Jerry. *Moneylove*. New York: Warner Books, 1979.

Hesse, Herman. *Siddhartha*. New York: New Directions Publishing, 1951.

215

Horney, Karen. *The Neurotic Personality of Our Time*. New York: W. W. Norton, 1937.

Leonard, George. *Education and Ecstasy*. New York: Delacorte Press, 1968.

May, Rollo. *The Courage to Create*. New York: Bantam Books, 1975.

May, Rollo. *Love and Will*. New York: Delta Books, 1969.

Napier, Augustus Y., with Carl A. Whitaker. *The Family Crucible*. New York: Bantam Books, 1979.

Rose, Phyliss. *Parallel Lives: Five Victorian Marriages*. New York: Alfred A. Knopf, 1984.

Watzlwick, Paul, John Weakland, and Richard Fisch. *Change: Principles of Problem Formation and Problem Resolution*. New York: W. W. Norton, 1974.

Index

217

219